Routledge Revivals

The Education of Children Engaged in Industry in England 1833-1876

Originally published in 1931, this title looks at the education received by children working in industry in England between 1833 and 1876. The industrial revolution created more demand for child labour than ever before, but there were few laws to protect the children involved. School was not compulsory for children until the 1880s, but there were new laws brought in and enforced to reduce the numbers of hours they were allowed to work in industry in 1833 and subsequently in 1844. This title deals with the education of children during that time and the implications of the laws introduced.

The Education of Children Engaged in Industry in England 1833-1876

Adam Henry Robson

Routledge
Taylor & Francis Group

First published in 1931
by Kegan Paul, Trench, Trubner & Co. Ltd

This edition first published in 2019 by Routledge
2 Park Square, Milton Park, Abingdon, Oxon OX14 4RN

and by Routledge
52 Vanderbilt Avenue, New York, NY 10017

Routledge is an imprint of the Taylor & Francis Group, an informa business

Publisher's Note
The publisher has gone to great lengths to ensure the quality of this reprint but
points out that some imperfections in the original copies may be apparent.

Disclaimer
The publisher has made every effort to trace copyright holders and welcomes
correspondence from those they have been unable to contact.

A Library of Congress record exists under LCCN: 31023006

ISBN: 978-0-367-13845-5 (hbk)
ISBN: 978-0-429-02885-4 (ebk)
ISBN: 978-0-367-13850-9 (pbk)

THE
EDUCATION OF CHILDREN
ENGAGED IN INDUSTRY
IN ENGLAND
1833—1876

BY
ADAM HENRY ROBSON
M.C., M.Sc., Ph.D.

LONDON
KEGAN PAUL, TRENCH, TRUBNER & CO., LTD.
BROADWAY HOUSE: 68-74 CARTER LANE, E.C.
1931

Thesis approved for the degree of Doctor of Philosophy in the University of London.

Printed in Great Britain by the DEVONSHIRE PRESS, *Torquay*

TO
V. M. R.
AND
V. M. R.

' The real problem as it presented itself to Englishmen in the Thirty Years of Peace was concerned with the rescue of children from premature wage-earning. The student of educational politics should attach more importance to the Factory Bills and the educational clauses attached to these measures than to the trifling grants which were approved . . . after 1832. The urgent problem which . . . had been stirring the public mind for many years was the oppression of children by the demands of industry for their labour. The system of English elementary education in its origin and in its developments right up to the Act of 1918 has been shaped predominantly by this issue. The school has been established and maintained just because attendance at school is presented as the only alternative to over pressure in the factory and on the farm.'—PROF. J. J. FINDLAY, *The Children of England* (1923).

AUTHOR'S ACKNOWLEDGMENTS

I wish to acknowledge with much gratitude the help and advice I have received during the preparation of this work from Professor J. Dover Wilson, Litt. D., King's College, London. To my friend, Mr. W. A. Dickins, I am greatly indebted for the assistance he has given me in reading the proofs and in preparing the index. I desire also to record my thanks to the Senate of London University for aiding the publication of the book from the Publication Fund of the University.

Lastly, I would acknowledge most gratefully the excellent facilities afforded me for consulting papers in the Library of the London School of Economics and Political Science.

A. H. ROBSON.

February, 1931

CONTENTS

THE EDUCATION OF CHILDREN
ENGAGED IN INDUSTRY IN ENGLAND

CHAPTER I

CHILD EMPLOYMENT IN FACTORIES UP TO 1831

ALTHOUGH the following pages will deal with the employment of children during the early days of the factory system, it would be outside the scope of the subject to give here any detailed account of the origin and growth of that system. A vast change in the textile industries began about the middle of the eighteenth century with the invention of mechanical means of performing operations which hitherto had been done mainly by hand, by operatives working in their own homes. The introduction of Hargreaves' spinning jenny, Arkwright's water frame, and Crompton's mule, together with the application at the end of the century of steam power to these machines, led to successive changes in the industries, the effect of which was to bring about the concentration of machinery in special buildings—workshops, mills and factories—and consequently the beginnings of the factory system.[1] The

[1] ' The leading feature of the industrial revolution was undoubtedly the establishment of large factories in which all the motive power was supplied by a single mechanism installed in the centre of the factory, and looked after by a large number of hands working under the supervision of one man.' *A History of the English People in* 1815. Halévy, p. 240.

evolution of similar conditions in weaving was much slower. There had indeed been no lack of inventions in this connection, but for a time at least it was found that these could be exploited by weavers continuing to work in their homes. Improvements in the power loom, however, and in the utilisation of steam power to operate it, gradually brought about a change to factory conditions in weaving operations also, and by 1833 the process of change from the domestic to the factory system, already complete as regards cotton, was advancing rapidly throughout the whole of the textile industries.[1] There remained, it is true, a considerable number of handloom weavers, who continued up to the middle of the nineteenth century to work at home, but their condition of life had been continuously declining, and, even before the year with which this book begins, was one of utter wretchedness.[2]

The early factories had been erected in districts where

[1] *Cf.* ' This class [the cotton trade] constitutes of itself about five-ninths of the whole population engaged in the entire manufactures of the Kingdom.' *The Manufacturing Population of England*, Gaskell, P. (1833), p. 9.

[2] As late as 1842, at the time of the investigations of the Children's Employment Commission, it was found that a large number of children were employed in handloom weaving at home. These children, wrote J. L. Kennedy, who was carrying out enquiries in Lancashire, were more to be commiserated than most of the operatives in large factories. ' I have frequently seen them at work in their cold, dark, damp cellars, without any fire or means of ventilation, and the atmosphere on entering the room, was literally foetid with the breath of the inmates . . , Many of them work from very early in the morning till late at night to make the smallest pittance. I have frequently been told by young boys in the trade that they have worked from five in the morning till twelve at night for many days without intermission . . . It is one of the unhappy cases which it is impossible to reach by legislation, and nothing remains but to warn the working classes to avoid entering upon an occupation which must ever entail upon them an inheritance of disease and wretchedness.' *Parl. Pap.* 1843, XIV (Report of the Commissioners), pp. B.40-1.

water power was readily obtainable.[1] These districts were sometimes away from centres of population, and consequently it had been necessary for the mill-owners to induce workers to migrate. A fruitful source of supply of labour was found in the destitute children of the parochial poor law authorities. To the latter, the 'new large-scale industries had come as a godsend'.[2] The children were drafted into the cotton mills in considerable numbers, and apprenticed to the age of 21, in the meantime being almost completely at the mercy of their employers. The tale of the oppression they often endured has frequently been told. Working long hours, living in overcrowded rooms, ill-fed, and often shamefully punished, their life was one of unending misery. 'Long hours and overworked children were certainly not confined to cotton-spinning', a leading historian has recently remarked, 'but there was a wholesaleness, a monstrosity, about the great cotton mills, which marked them down for public notice.'[3] As early as 1784, the attention of the Manchester magistrates had been called to the wretched condition of these children, by a serious outbreak of infectious fever in one of the factories.[4] But though the magistrates took

[1] 'In 1788 [southern Lancashire] contained more than forty spinning mills. This was due to the abundant water power, for the high hills on the south-east run very steeply across to the coast. Even though we can say that the geographical position and the climate, as well as the prosperity, of the port of Liverpool, favoured the growth of the cotton industry in Lancashire, yet it is the existence of streams providing the necessary power, which explains why the earliest factories grew up round Blackburn, Bury, Oldham and Manchester.' *Industrial Revolution in the Eighteenth Century*. Mantoux P. (English trans.), p. 253.

[2] *An Economic History of Modern Britain, the Railway Age*. Clapham, J. H., p. 371.

[3] Clapham, *op. cit.*, p. 184.

[4] *History of Factory Legislation*. Hutchins and Harrison, pp. 7 and 8.

B

some steps to bring to the notice of mill-owners the need for better sanitary conditions, the evils continued to grow rather than to diminish.[1]

In 1802, Sir Robert Peel, the father of the future Prime Minister, and himself a large cotton-mill owner, was the means of securing the passing of the first Act of Parliament to deal with this problem.[2] This *Act for the Preservation of the Health and Morals of Apprentices and others employed in Cotton and other Mills* enacted that an apprentice should not be compelled to work for more than twelve hours a day, exclusive of time for meals, and should not be compelled to work between the hours of 9 p.m. and 6 a.m. It provided also for the periodical white-washing of the walls

---

[1] A Manchester Board of Health, comprising persons interested in improving this state of affairs, was formed in 1795. They urged the need of legislation being passed to improve factory conditions. *Cf.* the following resolutions of this Board, which were later brought to the notice of the Select Committee on the State of Children Employed in Manufactories, 1816 (quoted from Hutchins and Harrison, *op. cit.*, pp. 10 and 11) :

' The untimely labour of the night, and the protracted labour of the day, with respect to children, not only tends to diminish future expectations as to the general sum of life and industry, by impairing the strength and destroying the vital stamina of the rising generation, but it too often gives encouragement to idleness, extravagance and profligacy in the parents who, contrary to the order of nature, subsist by the oppression of their offspring.

' It appears that the children employed in factories are generally debarred from all opportunities of education, and from moral and religious instruction.

' From the excellent regulations which subsist in several cotton factories, it appears that many of these evils may be in a considerable degree obviated ; we are therefore warranted by experience, and are assured we shall have the support of the liberal proprietors of these factories in proposing an application for parliamentary aid (if other methods appear not likely to effect the purpose). to establish a general system of laws for the wise, humane and equal government of all such works.'

[2] 42 Geo. III, c. 73.

and ceiling of the mill-rooms ; for better ventilation ; for the adequate clothing of the apprentices ; and for their religious instruction. It contained also a clause to provide for their education :

'Every such apprentice shall be instructed, in some part of every working day, in the usual hours of work, in Reading, Writing and Arithmetic, or either of them, according to the age and abilities of such apprentice, by some discreet and proper person, to be provided by the master or mistress of such apprentice, in some room or place in such mill or factory to be set apart for that purpose.'

Since the Act applied only to apprentices, employers were not slow to realise that they could avoid its restrictions by employing ' free ' child labour. And this became increasingly possible as population grew and families increased around the mills and, a little later, as the application of steam power to drive the mill machinery led to mills being erected in the towns, where child labour was more plentiful. But though beyond the law, these ' free ' children soon became the object of public apprehension, as the pauper children had been, and in 1815 Sir Robert Peel, influenced in this matter by Robert Owen,[1] again attempted to bring about an amelioration in the conditions of their life and work.[2] On 6th June 1815 he obtained

[1] *Cf.* the account given in *The Life of Robert Owen by Himself.* Bohn's Popular Library Edition, 1920, pp. 159 *et seq.*

[2] ' Gentlemen ', Peel remarked to the Select Committee appointed in the following year, ' if parish apprentices were formerly deemed worthy of the care of Parliament, I trust you will not withhold from the unprotected children of the present day an equal measure of mercy, as they have no masters who are obliged to support them in sickness or during unfavourable periods of trade.' *Select Committee on the State of Children Employed in Manufactories : Parl. Pap.* 1816, III, p. 367.

leave to bring in a Bill to amend the Act of 1802,[1] and proposed to extend the Act to all cotton, woollen, flax and other mills in which twenty or more persons under eighteen years of age were employed; to prohibit the employment of children under the age of ten years; to limit the hours of employment of anyone under eighteen to ten and a half per day, exclusive of time for meals and for instruction; to prevent night employment; and to provide that every child 'shall for the four first years after the time of their admission into any such mill . . . be instructed one half-hour in every working day, in Reading, Writing and Arithmetic '. In place of the J.P. and clergyman who under the Act of 1802 were to act as visitors to the mills to ensure that the law was carried out,[2] Peel now proposed that the Justices should appoint the Clerk of the Peace or his Deputy or 'one or more persons duly qualified, and not interested in or in any way connected with ' the mills to be visitors, to whom ' full and adequate compensation for their trouble and expense ' might be

[1] *Bill to preserve the health and morals of apprentices in cotton mills and other factories : Parl. Pap. 1814-15, II, p. 735.*

[2] This supervision had been quite neglected, as is shewn by the evidence of William David Evans, Barrister and Stipendiary Magistrate for Manchester, before the Select Committee on the State of Children Employed in Manufactories (1816) : On being asked whether he was ' apprised of the Bill passed for the government of apprentices in factories ', he replied, ' I was fully apprised of the existence of such an Act, but I believe I never read the contents of it till I read them yesterday in this room . . . I am sure it is not at present in operation in Lancaster ; nor, I believe, in Cheshire . . . It certainly is my intention to propose, at the Midsummer sessions, to execute that power that is there mentioned, of the appointment of inspectors ; another very important particular of the Act, in which I understand from the information of the clerk of the peace that the directions have not been complied with, is that of making a return of the cotton mills, and the number of apprentices employed in them.' *Parl. Pap.* 1816, III, p. 554.

paid out of the rates. It was clear, however, that Peel did not contemplate immediate legislation, for he suggested that ' during the recess, it [the Bill] might be circulated through the country, and receive proper amendments '. In the following year a Select Committee, with Sir Robert Peel as chairman, was appointed to inquire into the ' state of the children employed in the manufactories of the United Kingdom,' consideration of the Bill being deferred in the meantime.

The chief force behind the factory reform movement at this time was Robert Owen, the proprietor of the large cotton mills at New Lanark, in Scotland, who had proved in his own business that better conditions of employment, shorter hours of labour, and provision for the education and welfare of his employees were not only compatible with prosperity but promoted it, and who was inspired with zeal to see similar conditions obtaining elsewhere. ' The employer regards the employed as mere instruments of gain,' he wrote in 1815, ' while these acquire a gross ferocity of character, which, if legislative measures shall not be judiciously devised to prevent its increase, and ameliorate the conditions of this class, will sooner or later plunge the country into a formidable and perhaps inextricable state of danger.

' . . . The only mode by which these objects can be accomplished is to obtain an Act of Parliament :

' First,—To limit the regular hours of labour in mills of machinery to twelve per day, including one hour and a half for meals.

' Second,—To prevent children from being employed in mills of machinery until they shall be ten years old, or that they shall not be employed more than six hours per day until they shall be twelve years old.

'Third,—That children of either sex shall not be admitted into any manufactory,—after a time to be named, —until they can read and write in an useful manner, understand the first four rules of arithmetic, and the girls be likewise competent to sew their common garments of clothing.'[1]

Owen not only gave evidence before the Select Committee as to the beneficial effect of these arrangements at his own mills[2] but also organised the submission of the evidence in support of the proposals of Sir Robert Peel's Bill, for

[1] In *Observations of the Effect of the Manufacturing System*. See *A New View of Society and Other Writings*, by Robert Owen. (Everyman's Library Edition, 1927, pp. 124, 125).

[2] *Cf.* his description of the educational arrangements at his mills before the Committee on the Education of the Lower Orders (1816) : ' The children are received into a preparatory or training school at the age of three . . . In this training school the children remain for two or three years, according to their bodily strength and mental capacity ; when they have attained as much strength and instruction as to enable them to unite, without creating confusion with the youngest classes in the superior school, they are taught to read, write, account, and the girls in addition, to sew ; but the leading object in this more advanced stage of their instruction, is to form their habits and dispositions. The children generally attend this superior day school until they are ten years old ; and they are instructed in healthy and useful amusements for an hour or two every day, during the whole of this latter period. Among these exercises and amusements, they are taught to dance ; those who have good voices, to sing ; and those among the boys who have a natural taste for music, are instructed to play on some instrument. At this age, both boys and girls are generally withdrawn from the day school, and are put into the mills or to some regular employment. Some of the children, however, whose parents can afford to spare the wages which the children could now earn, continue them one, two, or three years longer in the day school, by which they acquire an education which well prepares them for any of the ordinary active employments of life. Those children who are withdrawn from the day school at ten years of age, and put into the mills or to any other occupation in or near the establishment, are permitted to attend, whenever they like, the evening schools . . . and it is found that out of choice about 400, on the average, attend every evening . . . 300 children attended the day school.' *Parl. Pap.* 1816, lV, *Minutes of Evidence*, pp. 240-1.

the form of which proposals Owen had been largely responsible. But faced with the strongest opposition from the manufacturers generally, Peel himself did not stand firmly enough by his proposals. Giving evidence before the Committee Peel at first suggested that the Bill should be amended by limiting its operation to ' the three great manufactures of the United Kingdom '—cotton, woollen and flax ; by making nine, instead of ten, years, the age under which employment should be prohibited ; by allowing employment for thirteen hours a day (including one and a half for meals and recreation) ; and by reducing the age of those to whom the provisions should apply from eighteen to sixteen years. The opposition, however, was too powerful even for this.[1] The inquiries of the Committee dragged on until the end of the session, when, however, they were still not completed, and no proper report as to the proceedings and findings of the Committee was made.

[1] One Manchester millowner even collected statistics and information for the Committee, which, he alleged, supported the view that the condition of the factory children was already superior to that of other children. Thus, the statement he obtained from one Sunday school read : ' The children that work in factories, we observe, are equally regular (or more so) in their attendance, more clean in their persons, more orderly in their conduct, and better clothed than those who do not. As far as we have observed, they enjoy as good health, though they do not look so well as other children.' Whilst from another Sunday school he obtained the report : ' Since the great exertions adopted through the Manchester and Salford districts, of Sunday schools for the last ten years, the children have, from the cleanliness requisite in attending these nurseries of piety, become more healthy than formerly ; the regulations and moral duties inculcated being cleanliness, steady and sober habits, regular attendance and virtue. . . . The school I have been employed in during the last ten years consists chiefly of children employed in factories ; and I can speak from experience, that they are more regular in attendance, more docile in behaviour, more tractable in disposition, and consequently more attentive to improvement.' *Select Committee on the State of Children Employed in Manufactories*. *Parl. Pap.* 1816, III, pp. 609, 610.

Further action in Parliament was not taken until the beginning of 1818, when Sir Robert Peel introduced another Bill, in which the proposals of the Bill of 1815 were watered down still further : the provisions of this new Bill were to apply to cotton factories only.

On 27th April 1818 Peel the younger, answering the argument that the education of the children was already satisfactorily provided for by the Sunday schools and the evening schools attached to them, said that these measures but ' proved to his mind the hardships to which [the children] were subjected. He learned with disgust that they were not sent to school to receive that instruction which might raise them above the machine at which they worked, till they had been exhausted by thirteen or fifteen hours of labour. . . . Was it not disgusting to see that education, which was intended to be the greatest of blessings, converted into a curse by this mode of compelling the children to try and avail themselves of it, after thirteen hours and a half of fatigue, when, throughout the day, labour had drained from them every spring of action that could refresh their faculties, and benumbed that elasticity of mind which could excite them in the pursuit of study ? '[1]

The Bill was eventually passed by the House of Commons, though not without meeting strong opposition, only to meet with still more formidable opposition in the House of Lords. The session ended with the consideration of the Bill in the Lords still unfinished ; and it remained to the next session, in 1819, to see it placed on the statute book.[2]

[1] *Hansard*, 1818, XXXVIII, p. 356.
[2] 59 Geo. III, c. 66.

Although this Act of 1819 left untouched all but the cotton mills, the conditions in the silk-throwing mills were perhaps even worse and those in the woollen mills no better. Moreover, a main defect of its provisions was that no adequate arrangements were authorised to ensure that it was complied with. This was calculated to render the measure from its inception practically a dead letter.[1] It was stated in 1825 by John Cam Hobhouse, Radical M.P. for Westminster, that only two convictions had ever taken place under the Act. ' In the best regulated mills the children were at present compelled to work twelve and a half hours a day,' Hobhouse told the House of Commons—the *best* regulated, be it noted—' and for three

[1] *Cf.* the reference to reports from visitors in 1823 and 1824 in the *Town Labourer* (Hammond, J. L.\, p. 169 : ' The Committee appointed for the hundred of Leyland reported to the Quarter Sessions at Preston that they have not found any instance whatsoever in which the Acts . . . have been observed either as respecting the employment of children being less than nine years of age, or as to whitewashing or ventilating the said manufactories.' *Cf.* also : ' In February 1823 he [Peel the younger] wrote to the clerks of the peace for the counties in which the cotton trade was chiefly located, demanding the names of all persons appointed as visiting magistrates to cotton mills under the Health and Morals of Apprentices Act. The inquiry reveals, as he probably expected, that the Act was very imperfectly enforced ; in some cases visitors had not been appointed for many years, in others never. The Secretary ordered that they should be appointed immediately, and the Act strictly observed in future. When the list of visiting magistrates was completed, Peel wrote to each individually, requesting them to report " whether you have any reason to believe that the provisions of the 59 Geo. III, 66 " (i.e. the Factory Act of 1819) " are materially transgressed with respect to hours of work, hours of meals, and the age of the children employed " . . . The replies are interesting, showing the disadvantages of the system of local inspection. Some visitors did excellent work, while other reports were of the most perfunctory nature. One magistrate was three months late in sending in his report, as he " had a painful sensation in his head." Another had not inspected at all, as he was not now resident in the district to which he had been appointed.' *Sir Robert Peel.* Ramsay, A. A. M. 1927), pp. 72 and 73.

or four days in the week were not allowed to go out of the
mills to get their meals, which they were obliged to take
off the floor of the mill, mingled with the dust and down
of the cotton.   In other mills they were forced to work
fifteen or sixteen hours a day.'[1] In this year (1825),
therefore, Hobhouse introduced a Bill to improve this
state of affairs. In a considerably amended form—
Hobhouse's proposal to reduce the hours of work of
children from twelve to eleven had to be abandoned—
it was passed during the summer.[2] The Act, however,
was hardly calculated to bring about any great change.
The justices were empowered to summon witnesses to give
evidence ; and mill proprietors were to be compelled to
keep a book for registering the entry of every child into
the mill.[3] But conditions remained very much what
they had been, and the problem of securing legislation
which would effectually mitigate them remained unsolved.
A further effort on the part of Hobhouse, in 1831, again
made little change.   His Bill sought to raise the age of
restricted employment from sixteen to eighteen years ;
to reduce the hours of work of children to eleven and a
half a day ; and to apply restriction to woollen,
worsted, linen and silk mills, as well as to cotton mills.
But only in securing the first of these objects was
the Bill successful.[4]   And none of the proposals introduced since Peel's Factory Bill of 1815 had made any

---

[1] *Hansard* 1825, XIII, p. 645.

[2] 6 Geo. IV, c. 63.

[3] But the Act provided that 'if the parent or guardian of a
child signs the book specifying that the child is of or above nine
years of age the proprietor is exempt from any prosecution in respect
of age.'

[4] 1 and 2 Will. IV, c. 39.

attempt to provide for the education of the children affected.[1]

Agitation, however, too formidable to be disregarded, was by this time spreading throughout the textile districts

[1] The activities of the National Society (a Church of England organisation founded in 1811) and of the British and Foreign School Society (1813) —the latter the successor of the undenominational Royal Lancasterian Institution (1808)—combined with private charity, had resulted in a considerable increase since the beginning of the century in the provision of schools throughout the country. But the school accommodation was still far short of what was needed. The Sunday school movement had made great strides since its beginning towards the end of the 18th century. Reading and writing, and often arithmetic, were taught at the Sunday schools, which constituted the chief means of education for a considerable part of the population. *Cf.* the following accounts given in *The Digest of Parochial Returns made to the Select Committee on the Education of the Poor* (*Parl. Pap.* 1819, IX) : ' In Leigh [Lancashire] there are numerous day schools, containing together 650 scholars ; and Sunday schools, in which 1881 children received instruction, and some dame schools . . . The poorer classes are liberally assisted in the education of their children '. ' In Ribchester, the poorer classes are entirely dispossessed of the means of educating their children, and it is only by means of a Sunday school they receive any instruction, though extremely desirous of being educated.' ' In Ainsworth, the poorer classes, which form a proportion of 19/20ths of the population, have no other means of education than the Sunday schools ; and from the numbers that attend it evidently appears that a particular desire exists among them, to have their children educated.' ' The poor class in Lees [near Ashton-under-Lyne] being generally weavers, are most desirous of obtaining instruction for their children, but being compelled to put them to labour at an early age, the only means they can avail themselves of are the Sunday schools. Were a capacious building erected in the centre of this chapelry, it would be available for the several purposes of a day school, an evening school, and also for a Sunday school, all of which are particularly wanted here.' ' The means of education in Leeds are very considerable, and well attended to ; but in the township they are deficient. The woollen manufacture in Armley affords so great a temptation, that parents are induced to employ their children at a very early age : consequently they can only take advantage of the Sunday schools.'

Cf. also the *Report from the Select Committee on the Education of the Poorer Classes in England and Wales* (1838) : ' Your Committee now turn to the state of Education in the large manufacturing and seaport towns, where the population has rapidly increased within the present century ;

of Lancashire and Yorkshire. Richard Oastler, a Tory land-agent, had inaugurated a campaign by writing a letter on 29th September 1830 to the leading Leeds newspaper, basing his observations on the current maxim that ' it is the pride of Britain that a slave cannot exist on her soil '. His revelation of the unimaginable truth regarding child employment in the mills caused a great sensation, and aroused on the one hand widespread enthusiasm among the workers, and on the other the fierce opposition of the mill owners.[1] Short-Time Committees were set up throughout the textile districts, with the object of undertaking propaganda and of bringing pressure on Members of Parliament to amend the law.

they refer for particulars to the Evidence taken before them, which appears to bear out the following results :

' 1st. That the kind of education given to the children of all working classes is lamentably deficient.

' 2nd. That it extends (bad as it is) to but a small proportion of those who ought to receive it.

' 3rd. That without some strenuous and persevering efforts be made on the part of the Government, the greatest evil to all classes may follow from this neglect.' *Parl. Pap.* 1837-38, VII, p. 163.

Possibly the position was different away from the newer industrial districts, e.g. of Lancashire and Yorkshire. ' If we could take the ordinary school in a moderate-sized village, or in a small town, where the population had not increased too rapidly for the school accommodation to keep pace with it, we should find a more satisfactory state of affairs than is generally imagined.' Sadler, M. E., in *Special Reports (Education Department),* ii, 450, quoted in *Education and Social Movements* 1700-1850. Dobbs, A.E. (1919), p. 160.

[1] ' The brave words of Richard Oastler rang forth undauntedly to the working classes of Yorkshire : " Let no promises of support from any quarter sink you into inactivity. Consider that you must manage this cause yourselves. Collect information and publish facts. Let your politics be : Ten hours a day and a time-book.' *English Social Reformers.* Gibbins, H. B. (1913), p. 122.

CHAPTER II

THE FACTORY ACT OF 1833

ON 15th December, 1831, Michael Thomas Sadler, M.P. for Newark and the spokesman in Parliament of the Short-Time Movement, sought to bring before Parliament a Bill to regulate the labour of children employed in mills and factories.[1] The preamble to the Bill was somewhat sweeping and provocative :

'Whereas it is necessary that the hours of labour of children and young persons employed in mills and factories, of whatever description should be regulated, inasmuch as it has of late become a practice in many such mills and factories to employ a great number of children and young persons of both sexes an unreasonable length of time, and late at night, and in many instances all night, to the great and manifest injury of the health and morals of such children and young persons . . .'

It was to apply to any cotton, woollen, worsted, hemp, flax, tow, linen or silk mills and factories. It proposed to prohibit the employment of children under nine years of age ; to limit the period of actual work between the ages of nine and eighteen years to ten hours daily, exclusive of time allowed for meals—with an abatement of two hours on Saturdays ; and to forbid all night work

[1] *Hansard*, 1831-32, IX, pp. 255-6.

15

under twenty-one years of age.[1] In moving the second reading of his Bill, on 16th March, 1832,[2] Sadler explained that these proposals were not all he would have liked to include ; he had, for instance, intended to provide for a remission of an hour a day for children under fourteen, or otherwise six hours on one day every week, for the purpose of ' affording those who are thus early and strangely forced into the market of labour some opportunity of receiving the rudiments of instruction and education, the expense of which upon the modern system would have been nothing, especially if shared between the mill-owner and the parish'.[3]   He had, however, refrained from making further provisions of a restrictive character in order, if possible, to secure the attainment of the main objects. The Bill was referred to a Committee of the House, of which Sadler was the Chairman and which met constantly up to the end of the Parliamentary session in August.[4]   A large number of operatives, including many children, were examined as to the hours of their employment and the nature of their work and the physical effects it produced.   A few mill-owners were interrogated too ; and the views of several medical men were heard.   It was shown conclusively that there existed a shocking state of overwork, resulting in excessive fatigue, ill-health and physical deformity.[5]   As regards education, scarcely any

[1] *Bill to regulate the labour of children and young persons in mills and factories : Parl. Pap.* 1831-32, II, 1.

[2] *Hansard,* 1832, XI, pp. 340-385.   [3] *Ibid.,* p. 375.

[4] *Report from Select Committee on the Bill to regulate the labour of children in mills and factories : Parl. Pap.* 1831-32, XV, 1.

[5] *Cf.* ' Before this committee there files a long procession of workers, men and women, girls and boys.   Stunted, diseased, deformed, degraded, each with the tale of his wronged life, they pass across the stage, a living picture of man's cruelty to man.' *The Town Labourer.* J. L. and B. Hammond, p. 171.

of the operatives appeared to have had any worth the name. To have begun work at seven, eight or nine years of age, with hours of employment from 5 or 6 a.m. to 9 p.m. (with a little time off for meals) was the common experience of the workpeople, children as well as adults. In such circumstances, it was natural that the children on their return home in the evenings should be too fatigued to receive instruction or attend school, even if facilities for this had existed. ' I have witnessed scores of times ', said one parent regarding his children, ' that they have been so fatigued when they came home, that they have let the vessel they have been holding in their hands fall on the floor ; they could not hold it in their hands, nature has been so weary and exhausted.'[1] Another witness produced letters from a number of teachers showing the impossibility of the children receiving any satisfactory instruction in the evenings. One of these teachers wrote :[2]

' I have taught a school for the last sixteen years in the immediate vicinity of a number of spinning mills, and during that time I have frequently had numbers of young persons there employed, attending my evening classes, of both sexes, and I feel no hesitation in saying, that I consider the long hours they are obliged to labour very injurious to their bodily health ; and as to making any improvement in learning, it is nearly impossible, as they are generally so fatigued by the labour of the day, as to fall asleep if not actually employed in receiving instruction. I have known instances of their being so exhausted as to hide themselves in the school, and fall asleep, and were only discovered by their parents coming

[1].*Ibid.*, p. 131.
[2] *Ibid.*, p. 358.

for the key, have searched the school, and found them sound asleep.'

Another teacher wrote :[1]

' I have frequently observed the languid state of those children when in school ; some of them, through the fatigue of the day, fall asleep when writing their copies ; others when learning to read, etc. ; it is therefore very difficult to communicate instruction to them.'

Several of the operatives and children examined had attended Sunday schools. The Sunday schools were free, whereas instruction in the evening schools had to be paid for. They were usually open on Sundays from 9 a.m. to 12 noon and from 1.30 to 4 p.m. and some were open again in the evening. Reading was taught ('from the alphabet to the Bible ', one Sunday school teacher put it), and sometimes writing and arithmetic ; and, of course, religious instruction was given also. But children who had been in mills for fifteen hours a day during the six preceding days could hardly be expected to be in a fit state, mental or physical, to profit much by such instruction as was given in the Sunday schools, the teachers in which were usually workpeople who themselves had had a very scanty education.

Parliament was dissolved in August 1832, before the hearing of all the evidence was completed. Lord Morpeth, one of the members of Sadler's Committee, stated in the House of Commons the following year that it had been an arrangement, to which Sadler and the Committee generally were parties, that Sadler should first call his evidence and go through his case, and that then the opponents of the Bill should call and go through theirs. The session had ended just as Sadler's case was concluded and before

[1] *Ibid.*, p. 358.

that of his opponents had been begun.[1] In the new
Parliament which assembled in January 1833, Sadler
failed to secure re-election.[2] His place as the leader of the
movement for shorter hours in the factories was taken by
Lord Ashley,[3] who early in the session introduced a Bill
which was substantially the same as that of Sadler. Though

[1] *Hansard*, 1833, XV, p. 391.

[2] He was defeated at Leeds by Macaulay. In 1834 he stood for
Huddersfield but was again unsuccessful. His health was by this time
failing, largely because of the strain of his labours in connection with the
collection of evidence for the Select Committee, and he died the following
year, at the age of 55 years.

[3] Anthony Ashley Cooper, subsequently seventh Earl of Shaftesbury.
Born in 1801, and succeeded to the title of Lord Ashley in 1811. Educated
at Harrow and at Christ Church, Oxford, obtaining a first class in classics
in 1822. Entered Parliament in 1826, as member for Woodstock, the
pocket borough of the Marlborough family. In 1830 he was returned for
Dorchester, and from the following year to 1846 he sat for the county of
Dorset. In 1851, he succeeded to the earldom. He held a minor office in
1828, and again in 1834 ; but he then deliberately sacrificed a political
career, for which his ability, connections, and high character might have
secured him the highest places, in order to be in an independent position,
to promote the cause of social reform. His ardent pursuit of the object
of the reform of working conditions in factories and in collieries and mines,
are indicated in the following pages. In addition to factory reform, his
name is intimately associated with the protection of lunatics, the abolition
of slavery, the establishment of ragged schools, and the Climbing Boys' Act.
His interest in the factory question was first aroused at the time mentioned above. His own description of the matter is as follows : ' In the
autumn and winter of 1832 I read incidentally in *The Times* some extracts
from the evidence taken before Mr Sadler's Committee. I had heard nothing of the question previously, nor was I even aware that an inquiry had
been instituted by the House of Commons. Either the question had made
very little stir, or I had been unusually negligent in Parliamentary business.
I suspect the first to have been the true cause, for it had been an active
session, and I had taken my full share in the activity of it. I was astonished
and disgusted ; and knowing Sadler to be out of Parliament (for he had
been defeated at Leeds), I wrote to him to offer my services in presenting
petitions, or doing any other small work that the cause might require.'
Quoted from Hodder's *Life and Work of the Earl Shaftesbury* in *Lord
Shaftesbury*. Hammond, J. L. and B. (1923), p. 20.

there were numerous petitions in support of the Bill presented to the new House, the mill-owners were mobilising their influence and their supporters with a view to securing the appointment of a commission to take further evidence. On 3rd April, 1833, Wilson Patten, one of the members for Lancashire, acting on behalf of the Association of Master Manufacturers, brought forward a motion to secure this object. He declared that Sadler's Committee had proceeded in a very partial manner ; thus, he alleged, the persons to whom the selection of witnesses was entrusted had been strictly cautioned not to send up any person on whom they could not rely ; 51 out of the 80 witnesses had been from Leeds and its neighbourhood, and hence the Committee's inquiries had not been really representative ; there was proof of the incorrectness and even falsehood of a great part of the evidence that had been given (in one case, the shocking deformity of the witness had been due not, as had been stated, to work in factories, but to injuries received in a wrestling match). The Government of the day favoured the proposal, and the motion was carried by a majority of one vote.[1] The Commission was appointed immediately, and consisted of fifteen members, of whom three—Thomas Southwood Smith, Thomas Tooke and Edwin Chadwick[2]—were

[1] *Hansard* 1833, XVII, pp. 79-113.

[2] Edwin Chadwick (1800-1890). A friend and pupil of the Mills and of Jeremy Bentham, becoming literary secretary to the latter. Appointed an Assistant Poor Law Commissioner in 1832, and Secretary of the Poor Law Board, which was set up under the Poor Law Amendment Act 1834. Among his later activities were his work on a Commission to consider the establishment of an efficient constabulary force in England and Wales, and on a Royal Commission to inquire into the sanitary condition of Great Britain. Chadwick was mainly responsible for the drafting of the Reports issued by these Commissions. His official career came to an end in 1854, but throughout the remainder of his life he continued to take a

appointed to organise the inquiry and frame a report. The instructions issued by these three, on 25th April, 1833, to the district and medical commissioners[1] were wide in scope and liberal in intention. 'The present Inquiry', they stated, 'embraces the whole subject of the labour of children, as now enforced in the various mills and factories, or places of work, throughout the country. It . . . will comprehend every description of manufacture in which the labour of children forms an important or essential part of the whole labour employed . . . It should be distinctly understood that the Inquiry is in no respect to be narrowed to the views of any class, or any party or interest. Nor are any prior measures, or proceedings having relation to such measures, to be considered in any other point of view than as part of the means for rendering the present Inquiry, or any measures which may be recommended in consequence of it, as complete and satisfactory as possible.' Among the detailed heads of Inquiry the instructions mentioned specifically, ' Whether the children are uneducated and whether their want of education results directly from the nature of their employment.' And again, ' Whether, if the employment of children of tender age, during limited hours, be unavoidable, or be beneficial, all circumstances considered, any securities can be taken for the education of these children previously to or during their employment in factories, or what specific

great interest in many questions of government and social conditions. ' A dominating personality, whose strong will, knowledge and forceful character are impressed on every page of the Sanitary and Poor Law Legislation of the nineteenth century.' *Sir Edwin Chadwick*, Marston, M. (1925), p. 30

[1] One Medical and two Civil Commissioners were appointed to each of the four districts into which the country was divided for the purpose of the Inquiry.

measures can be recommended to the Legislature or suggested to the local communities for the improvement of the moral and social condition of the persons employed in the several branches of manufacture in question . . .'[1]

The Commissioners worked with great vigour and speed, with the result that the Central Board of the Commission were able to submit a *First Report* on 25th June, 1833, little more than two months after their appointment. They found that whilst the greater number of factories did not employ children until nine years of age, in many instances children of seven and eight were taken on, and it was not uncommon to find them employed at six years of age. In some rare cases the children began to work at five years.[2]

As regards the physical effects of employment, they wrote : ' Whether the factory be in the pure air of the country, or in the large town ; under the best or the worst management ; and whatever be the nature of the work, whether light or laborious ; or the kind of treatment, whether considerate and gentle or strict and harsh ; the account of the child, when questioned as to its feelings of fatigue, is the same[3] . . . That the excessive fatigue, privation of sleep, pain in various parts of the body, and swelling of the feet experienced by the young workers, coupled with the constant standing, the peculiar attitude of the body, and the peculiar motions of the limbs required in the labour of the factories, together with the elevated temperature and the impure atmosphere in which that

[1] *First Report from Commissioners relative to the employment of children in factories : Parl. Pap.* 1833, XX, pp. 79-85.

[2] *Ibid.*, p. 19.

[3] *Ibid.*, p. 30.

labour is often carried on do sometimes ultimately terminate in the production of serious, permanent and incurable disease, appears to be well established.'[1]

From the same evidence, the Commissioners considered, in the great majority of cases the long hours and the physical strain of the work incapacitated the children from receiving instruction. The children seen by the Commissioners had invariably stated that they were too much fatigued to attend school in the evening, even when a school was provided for them—though the report added that the evidence of other witnesses both as to the capacity of the children for receiving instruction and as to their actual state in regard to education, was conflicting.[2]

In the evidence collected by the District Commissioners a few instances occur of care and interest being shown by mill-owners for the education of the children. Thus, John Marshall, M.P., of Marshall and Co., Leeds, informed the Commissioners that since the beginning of the year (1833) such children between nine and eleven years of age as they employed worked in the mill one half of the day and attended the company's school during the other portion of the day. 'We gave them 1/6 per week, out of which they had to pay 1d., 2d. or 3d. per week. The half fee for learning to read, 1d. ; read and write, 2d. ; or read, write and account, 3d., respectively.'[3]

This particular company had, in fact, taken an interest

---

[1] *Ibid.*, p. 33.

[2] *Ibid.*, p. 33.

[3] *Ibid.*, p. 1123. There was also a small library of books suitable for children attached to the school. Factories Inquiry Commission, *Supplementary Report : Parl. Pap.* 1834, XIX, p. 371. (*Cf.* also an account given by Mr Marshall before the Select Committee on Manufactures, Commerce and Shipping : *Parl. Pap.* 1833, VI, pp. 166-7.)

in the education of their workpeople for some years past. An evening school had been maintained since 1824 for ' hands from the factory, of all ages. We have eight at this time,' said the master of the school. ' When they have advanced as far as vulgar fractions, we consider that sufficient, and they make way for others. The admission to the evening school is a matter of favour, and the hands consider it a great privilege, and attend with great readiness. They consist principally of persons above the age of 14 ; some upwards of 30.'[1] Anthony R. Strutt, of the Belper and Milford Mills, Derby, informed the Commissioners that his firm already required all children, before being admitted to the mill, to have attended an elementary school of their own attached to the works. As to subsequent education, he added, ' All the boys that leave work on Saturdays at four o'clock we compel to attend school for about a couple of hours, not only for their improvement, but to prevent the mischief which we found before the adoption of this regulation they were apt to get into from mere wantonness . . . All the young persons under twenty are expected to attend Sunday schools '.[2] Thomas Ashton, the proprietor of a mill at Hyde, had himself built a school in which, he said, ' 640 children are instructed on Sundays, in reading, writing and arithmetic. There is a library connected with it in which the operatives frequently read after the conclusion of their work.' He had also provided an infants' school, in which there were upwards of 200 children ; and there were evening classes held twice weekly ' in which several of the children are educated in a superior manner '.[3] A mill owner at Stroud informed the Commissioners that he

[1] *Ibid.*, p. 579.   [2] *Ibid.*, p. 1122.   [3] *Ibid.*, p. 833.

had established an infants' school in the neighbourhood, adding : ' To encourage the parents to send their children to this school, I promise such children the preference of employment in the factory when fresh children are taken on.'[1] ' I give every encouragement to the education of the children in my employment,' said a mill owner at Taunton ; but he did not specify in what manner, except that he was in the habit of giving religious tracts as a reward for good conduct. ' I have found no stimulus to exertion so effectual as the hope of getting one of these tracts,' he remarked.[2] A master clothier at Trowbridge stated that he had contributed within the last two years £100 towards the erection of the ' British ' school in the town. He also subscribed to the infant school and to the Sunday school. A workman, however, from this employer's mill—selected at hazard by the Commissioners during their visit to the mill—stated that his three children in the mill were usually employed for thirteen hours a day exclusive of meals, and when they left off work they seemed very weary and often fell asleep instead of eating their supper. When asked why he did not make them work fewer hours he replied that it was because the master's demands would not allow of it.[3] The proprietor of the mills of Henry and Edmund Ashworth, cotton spinners, Turton, near Bolton, told the Commissioners that there was a school on the premises ' for children under nine years of age, conducted by a young woman of superior habits of life, who receives the whole of her support from the parents or friends of the children.' There was also an evening school attended by children and young persons who worked in the mill. ' After finishing their work in

[1] *Ibid.*, p. 933.   [2] *Ibid.*, p. 971..   [3] *Ibid.*, p. 995

the evening, they wash, and attend school for about three quarters of an hour, and mutually instruct each other before they retire to their families.'[1] It is difficult to think that the children can have greatly profited by the arrangements made in this latter case.

In the report of the Central Board attention was directed to the fact that in the Bill of Lord Ashley no provision had been made for assigning any part of the time of the children, either before or after their hours of work, for their own benefit, or for their education ' elementary or moral '.[2] They accordingly recommended that three or four hours a day should be given to education, and that as a means of securing this, every child on entering a factory should be required to produce a ticket certifying that such portion of their time had been spent in school. A system of employment by relays was recommended, under which children employed in the afternoon would attend school during the morning of the same day, and those employed in the morning would attend in the afternoon of the same day.[3] As regards hours of employment, the Commissioners proposed that children under nine years of age should not be employed at all in mills and factories, that until the beginning of the fourteenth year the daily hours of labour should not exceed eight, and that night work (i.e. between ten o'clock at night and five in the morning) should not be allowed.[4] To ease the position, both for the employers as regards obtaining the requisite number of ' hands ' and for the operatives as regards a sudden reduction in the family earnings, they suggested that the limitation to eight hours should, in the

[1] Ibid., p. 1103.   [2] Ibid., p. 38.
[3] Ibid., pp. 71, 72.   [4] Ibid., p. 56.

first instance, be applied only to children up to the commencement of the twelfth year ; that this limitation should
take effect in about six months after the passing of the
Bill, and should be extended, by intervals of six or twelve
months each, to children under the thirteenth and the
fourteenth year of age respectively.

Several prominent manufacturers had represented to the
Commissioners that the only certain method of ensuring
compliance with any legislative measures on this subject
would be by the appointment of officers charged with the
powers and duties requisite to enforce them.   The necessity
of this had been most urgently stated by those manufacturers who had chiefly in view the restriction of the hours
of labour in other factories to the level of their own.   In
their report the Commissioners remarked, with a touch
of irony perhaps, that the necessity of this must be admitted
when it was recollected that the proposed measures related
solely to children and were not directly conducive to the
immediate interests either of the master manufacturers
or of the operatives, and were not therefore likely to receive
' continuous and voluntary support '.   They accordingly
recommended the appointment by the Government of
three inspectors ' to go circuits of the chief manufacturing
districts, at intervals as short as may be practicable. . .
For this purpose the inspector should have the right of
entering all manufactories where children are employed . .
he should also have the cognisance of the arrangements
for the education of the children employed.   He should
have power to hear and determine all complaints of
infraction of the provisions of the law . . . and fine for
neglect.   It should be the duty of the inspectors to meet
on a board, to report periodically to the Government for

the use of the legislature as to their proceedings and as to any amendments of the law which they might find requisite. . . .'[1]

The Bill which Lord Ashley had introduced earlier in the year and in connection with which it had been decided to appoint the Factories Inquiry Commission, had followed Sadler's Bill of the preceding year in proposing the abolition of the employment of children under nine years in cotton, woollen, worsted, flax, hemp, tow, linen, lace, netting, weaving or silk mills or factories ; a limit of ten hours daily for the employment of all persons under eighteen years ; and the prohibition of night work for all under the age of twenty-one years.[2] On 5th July, 1833, i.e. only a few days after the Commission had reported, Lord Althorp, the Chancellor of the Exchequer, in moving that Lord Ashley's Bill be referred to a Select Committee of the House,[3] declared the attitude of the Government. It was clearly far from favourable in many ways to the object which Lord Ashley and the reformers had in view. By increasing the power of foreigners to compete in the British market, Lord Althorp thought, the effects of the Bill might be found very disastrous. He was quite willing, ' with the present feeling in the country and with the excitement which so generally prevailed ', to admit that some protection of children was necessary. But to say that protection should necessarily extend to persons who were masters of their own time (among whom he included all who were not under their fourteenth year) was to broach a proposition to which he hoped Parliament would never assent. He

[1] *Ibid.*, p. 72.

[2] *Bill to regulate the labour of children in mills and factories :   Parl. Pap.* 1833, II, p. 263.

[3] *Hansard* 1833, XIX, pp. 220-3.

accordingly proposed that a Select Committee should be appointed and that it should be an instruction to them that children under fourteen years should not be subjected to labour for more than eight hours a day, but that for those beyond that age the existing law regarding children employed in cotton mills should not be altered. He conceded that it might well be a question whether the existing Act might not very properly be extended to other than cotton factories.

In any legislation upon this subject, Lord Althorp went on to say, there was one great object to be kept in view, namely, the promotion of education. It must be evident that as children in factories were kept constantly employed throughout the day, it was impossible that they could acquire education, and it should therefore be seen that in any measure on the subject, care was taken that an interval at a reasonable period of the day should be reserved for their education. Further, he continued, the main difficulty in all such measures as the present was means for carrying the law into effect. It was notorious that although in cotton mills laws were in force for restricting the hours of labour, they were seldom, if ever, carried into effect. In Lord Ashley's Bill there were no provisions for that purpose, and he therefore proposed that the Select Committee should be instructed to ascertain the expediency of a system of inspection throughout the mills where children were employed.

This proposal to refer the Bill to a Select Committee was vigorously opposed by Lord Ashley.[1] The omissions as regards education and inspection were due merely to his not having wanted to give additional offence to the

[1] For debate see *ibid.*, pp. 224-254.

employing interests. Of course, he readily concurred with these parts of the Government's proposals. He succeeded in carrying a majority of the House with him ; and a fortnight later his Bill came before the House for detailed discussion. On this occasion, however, he soon encountered unsurmountable opposition. On the second clause of Ashley's Bill, limiting the hours of employment of all persons under eighteen to ten a day, Lord Althorp moved to substitute thirteen for eighteen years, and carried his motion by the overwhelming majority of 238 to 93.[1] In view of the position Lord Ashley had taken up, this was a vital blow at his measure, and, realising that he could not now hope for the success of his own measure, he surrendered the Bill into the hands of the Government.

The Government lost no time in amending it so as to bring it into line with their views, as to which they were mainly guided by the recommendations of the Factories Inquiry Commission. On the amended Bill coming before the House on 9th August, 1833, Lord Althorp briefly explained the provisions. No children under fourteen years of age should work more than eight hours a day ; those between thirteen and eighteen years should not exceed 69 hours work in the week—twelve hours a day with nine on Saturdays ; no children should on any account be employed under the age of nine years. These arrangements would be secured by the appointment of inspectors in such a way that no evasion would take place. Provisions were made regarding the education of the children. As regards this last, an important clause was included in the Bill[2] to secure the establishment of the necessary schools.

[1] *Ibid*, p. 913.
[2] *Bill to regulate the labour of children in mills and factories : Parl. Pap.* 1833, II, p. 281.

' Wherever it shall appear to any inspector that a new or additional school is necessary or desirable to enable the children employed in any factory to obtain the education required by this Act, such inspector is hereby authorised and required to establish or procure the establishment of such school by contract or otherwise ; and if the deduction hereinbefore authorised at the rate of one penny out of every shilling from the weekly wages of such children shall be insufficient to pay the expenses of such school, the employer or employers of such children shall pay the deficiency, each in the ratio of the number of children in their employment, which deficiency shall be assessed by and paid to the inspector ; and every sum so paid by any employer may be deducted by such employer out of the Poor-rates which shall next become due from such employer in respect of his factory ; and if such payment shall exceed the amount of the Poor-rates so due from such employer, the excess shall be reimbursed to him out of the Poor-rates of the town, parish or place in which such factory is rated ; and every overseer of such town, parish or place is hereby required to reimburse such employer accordingly.' Unfortunately this important provision was modified in the House of Lords in such a way as seriously to affect the value of the educational results which the Act might have led to. The authority proposed to be given to the inspectors to require the employers to defray the cost of providing schools—apart from the children's contribution of one penny out of each shilling of their wages—was deleted. They were authorised to procure the establishment of schools, but given no power to raise the money necessary for the purpose ! A further amendment of considerable importance was made. The Bill as passed in the Commons empowered the inspectors to dismiss a schoolmaster or schoolmistress deemed by them to be incompetent, or in any way unfit for the performance of the duties of that office. This provision, however, was deleted in the upper House, the power of the inspectors being limited to disallowing the payment of a sum from the children's wages to the schoolmaster or schoolmistress.

It may be convenient to give here the actual wording of the educational clauses as they were finally passed :[1]

' 20. From and after the expiration of six months from the passing of this Act every child hereinbefore restricted to the performance of forty-eight hours labour in any one week shall, so long as such child shall be within the said restricted age, attend some school to be chosen by the parents or guardians of such child, or such school as may be appointed by any inspector in case the parents or guardians of such child shall omit to appoint any school, or in case such child shall be without parents or guardians ; and it shall be lawful, in such last-mentioned case, for any inspector to order the employer of any such child to make a deduction from the weekly wages of such child as the same shall become due, not exceeding the rate of one penny in every shilling to pay for the schooling of such child ; and such employer is hereby required to pay the sum so deducted according to the order and direction of such inspector.

' 21. After the expiration of six months from the passing of this Act it shall not be lawful to employ or continue to employ in any factory or mill any child

[1] 3 and 4 Will. IV, c. 103.

restricted by this Act to the performance of forty-eight hours of labour in any one week, unless such child shall, on Monday in every week next after the commencement of such employment, and during every succeeding Monday or other day appointed for that purpose by an inspector, give to the factory master or proprietor, or to his agent, a schoolmaster's ticket or voucher, certifying that such child has for two hours at least for six out of seven days of the week next preceding attended his school, excepting in cases of sickness, to be certified in such manner as such inspector may appoint, and in the case of any holiday, and in case of absence from any due cause allowed by such inspector, or by any Justice of the Peace in the absence of the inspector ; and the said last-mentioned ticket shall be in such form as may be settled by any inspector.

' 22. Wherever it shall appear to any inspector that a new or additional school is necessary or desirable to enable the children employed in any factory to obtain the education required by this Act, such inspector is hereby authorised to establish or procure the establishment of such school

' 23. If upon any examination or inquiry any inspector shall be of opinion that any schoolmaster or schoolmistress is incompetent or in any way unfit for the performance of the duties of that office, it shall and may be lawful for such inspector to disallow and withhold the orders for any payment or any salary to such schoolmaster or schoolmistress as hereinbefore provided.'

The Act generally was to come into operation on 1st January, 1834, but its provisions restricting the hours of work of children were to come into force by stages, namely, six weeks after the passing of the Act—children under eleven years of age ; after eighteen months, children under twelve ; after thirty months, children under thirteen. The Act applied to children employed in cotton, woollen, worsted, hemp, flax, tow, and linen mills or factories, but not to lace mills. As regards silk mills, children under thirteen years were allowed to work ten hours a day and consequently they remained outside the scope of the educational clauses of the Act.[1]

The first inspectors appointed were Leonard Horner (who had been one of the Commissioners of the Factories Inquiry Commission), Thomas Jones Howell, Robert Rickards, and Robert J. Saunders. The districts assigned to the inspectors were as follows :

Mr Horner.—Scotland and the northern half of Ireland, together with Northumberland, Durham, Cumberland and Westmorland.

Mr Rickards.—Yorkshire, Lancashire and Cheshire, together with the northern parts of Derbyshire and Staffordshire and the counties along the northern coast of Wales.

---

[1] Discussion of the measure in the House of Commons had ended on 13th August 1833. Three days later Lord Althorp moved that a sum of £20,000 be granted in aid of the erection of schools for ' the education of the poorer classes '—to which the House agreed. There is nothing, however, in the record of the discussion that took place to indicate that there was any connection between this action and the proposal to make school attendance compulsory on factory children. The latter proposal was not to come into effect until 1st March 1834 (and then only as regards children under 11 years), and though opponents of the measure had declared that many of the children affected would be discharged by their employers, the extent to which this would be so could not be accurately known. It seems unlikely, therefore, that the possibility of these children being thrown out of employment influenced the House to any noticeable extent in the decision above mentioned.

Mr Howell.—The southern half of Ireland, Wales (except for the northern strip assigned to Mr Rickards), and the west midland counties of England—Staffordshire, Herefordshire, Worcestershire, Warwickshire and Gloucestershire.

Mr Saunders.—Eastern, southern and south-western England.

The inspectors[1] were required by the Act to keep full records of all their visits and proceedings, and to report separately to the Government (the Secretary of the Home Department) three months after taking up their appointments and twice yearly afterwards ; to meet twice at least in every year with a view to securing as much uniformity of practice as was expedient and practicable, and to present a joint report on such occasions for the Secretary of State.

The first communications from the inspectors, written at the end of 1833 after a preliminary survey of their districts and before the Act had actually come into operation, were not very encouraging. ' I have found an almost universal admission of the necessity of something being done for the better education of the children employed in factories ', wrote Horner[2] (26th December 1833) ; ' but

---

[1] Each of whom received a salary of £1,000 a year, to include travelling expenses. A number of superintendents (assistants to the inspectors) were also appointed at salaries varying from £250 to £350 a year. *Return of the names of the inspectors appointed to superintend the factories of the United Kingdom. Parl. Pap.* 1834, XLIII, p. 421.

[2] Leonard Horner (1785-1864), as will be seen from the following pages, played an important part in the work of factory inspection and in the promotion of education for factory children. The son of an Edinburgh linen factory owner, he studied science at Edinburgh University. Becoming a partner in his father's business, he went to London in 1804. Through the influence of his brother, who was one of the founders of the *Edinburgh*

D

I have found also an universal feeling that the education clause of the Act, as it now stands, is utterly impracticable; and I am persuaded that if it is attempted to put it into force, the manufacturers, however reluctantly, will certainly dismiss every child liable to the restrictions.'[1]　In his first half-yearly report (July 1834) he wrote that in no part of his district had he found the educational enactments complied with. The difficulties, he pointed out, were many. Very few mills were situated near a school which was open at hours when the factory children could attend —that was, early in the morning or late in the afternoon. If the system of ' relays ' was adopted, and the children divided into three sets, two sets being always in the mill and one at school, it would require the school to be open, allowing for meal times and for changing clothes, from about seven in the morning till five in the afternoon, which was rarely if ever the case.[2]　Again, the factory children must go to school in their working clothes, for they had not the time, nor could they afford, to change. The schoolmasters, however, did not like to receive them, nor would the factory children go in that attire to mix with other children better dressed. There was, further, no obligation on the part of the schoolmaster to take the trouble of making out the certificates, and some, in fact,

Review, and of his own interest in geology, he soon got in touch with scientific and literary circles. Became associated with the Geological Society in 1808, and was admitted a Fellow of the Royal Society in 1813. Returned to Edinburgh for business reasons, and became prominent as a Whig politician and an educational reformer. In 1827, Horner was invited to London to assist in organising the London Institution, and in 1828 became Warden of the London University at its opening. After serving on the Factories Inquiry Commission in 1833, he became one of the first factory inspectors, and continued as such until his retirement in 1858.

[1] *Parl. Pap.* 1834, XLIII, p. 427.　　　[2] *Ibid.*, p. 435.

had already refused to do so. The only remedy seemed to
be to have schools attached to the factories.[1] Howell,
reporting at the same time (July 1834), wrote that in
only two out of 330 establishments in his district had the
system of working by relays been attempted, in order
to retain in employment and enforce the education of
children under eleven years of age. There had been a
general discharge from employment of the children to
which the educational clauses applied.[2] Rickards (Lancashire and Yorkshire) expressed himself in still more
sweeping terms. With the exception of three mill owners
(Marshall, of Leeds ; Thomas Ashton, of Hyde ; and
Birley, of Manchester), who already had had schools
attached to their mills, the unanimous voice of the whole
district was to the effect that it would be impossible to
secure a sufficient number of ' young hands ' for the system
of relays and that there would be no alternative to dis-
charging all who were affected by the educational clauses
of the Act.[3] ' The utter impracticability of the schooling
clauses being attended to by the masters of the mills, or
being attended to by me ', he wrote (December 1833),
' is so obvious, that should this matter be hereafter called
in question, I trust I shall stand excused for dispensing
with their observance, at all events in cases where proof
to demonstration of this impracticability should be found
to exist.'[4] This attitude perhaps showed insufficient
determination on Rickards' part to ensure that the law
was carried into effect, and it is hardly surprising that his
tenure of the appointment was brief.

In their first joint report (July 1834) the inspectors went

[1] *Ibid.*, p. 435.　　[2] *Ibid.*, p. 446.
[3] *Ibid.*, p. 447.　　[4] *Ibid.*, p. 451.

so far as to express the view that it would be expedient to allow children of eight years to work in the mills, as they were inclined to think that in a great many cases these children would have ' both their health and morals less exposed to injury than in their ordinary course of living out of it '. They pointed out, too, that the object of the Act was materially counteracted by the power of the parents to find other employment for their children, in trades other than those subjected to restriction of hours and compulsory education ; and further, that so long as the 22nd clause, which dealt with the establishment of schools but did not effectively empower the inspector to procure their establishment, remained inoperative, the experiment of combining a system of education with factory employment could not have a fair trial.[1]

A census taken in the spring of 1835 of the number of persons employed in the mills and factories of the United Kingdom to which the Act applied resulted in the following figures for the number of children :[2]

District of	9 years	10 years	11 years	12 years	13 years
Mr Rickards	2,541	3,778	9,028	25,588	19,309
Mr Saunders	472	746	1,069	2,413	1,936
Mr Horner	227	495	1,065	6,036	4,494
Mr Howell	141	188	443	1,830	1,533
Total	3,381	5,207	10,705	35,867	27,272

[1] *Ibid.*, p. 492.

[2] Persons employed in the various mills and factories of the United Kingdom, *Parl. Pap.* 1836, XLV, p. 51. The number of children under 14 years of age employed in *cotton* factories *in England* at the time of the Factories Inquiry Commission had been stated by the Commissioners to be 24,665 boys and 19,038 girls. Factories Inquiry Commission, *Supplementary Report : Parl. Pap.* 1834, XIX, p. 441.

On 1st March. 1835, the additional restriction on the employment of children between eleven and twelve came into operation. The reports of this year, if not quite so devoid of hope for the successful working of the Act as those of the first year, continued to emphasise the failure of the effort made and the difficulty of the task. The prospect, too, of the further extension of the Act, in the following year, to children between twelve and thirteen years filled the inspectors with apprehension. Rickards, impressed by the ' invincible repugnance to the schooling sections ' found by him throughout Lancashire and Yorkshire, urged that a short Act should be passed ' to suspend the operation of the clause alluded to . . . and also the schooling clauses, until leave be given to consider the Act generally.'[1] Saunders found a few mills where schools had been established and the attendance regularly enforced, and from these he had received ' gratifying assurances that the improvement effected was evident and considerable ' ; but for the greater part, the children affected by the education provisions had continued to be excluded from the mills.[2] Horner found the prejudices against the system of working the children in relays, with consequent arrangements for their education, were beginning to give way, and at the end of the year he had in his district 65 mills, with 776 children affected, where it was in operation.[3]

In 1836 a determined attempt was made in Parliament to secure a modification of the Act so as to render it inapplicable to children between twelve and thirteen years

---

[1] *Reports of Factory Inspectors, Parl. Pap.* 1836, XLV., pp. 161, 162.
[2] *Ibid.*, p. 166.
[3] *Ibid.*, p. 167.

of age.   On 15th March, 1836,[1] a fortnight after the clause
limiting the hours of employment of children of twelve
years and providing for their education during two hours
a day came into effect, the Government introduced a
Bill to amend the Act so far as it affected these children.[2]
Such children, Poulett Thomson, the President of the
Board of Trade, told the House, might fairly be considered
capable of deciding for themselves.   He made considerable
use of the fact that the inspectors had ' made an unanimous declaration that they had found it almost
impossible to enforce the law as it had stood since 1st
March last.'   The employers, too, had said in no uncertain
fashion that if the clause referred to were allowed to
continue law, the inevitable consequence would be that
all children between the ages of twelve and thirteen would
be thrown out of employment ;   and thus, he said, it
became a matter of common humanity to revise the law
and save the parents from being deprived of the children's
earnings.[3]   Lord Ashley was the principal opponent of
the measure, and there was a considerable and powerful
body of opinion behind him.   He rested his case mainly
on the physical hardship entailed by the long hours of
employment to which these children would be subjected
if the Bill were passed, but he referred also to the need of
providing for their education.   He was perhaps more
concerned with their religious than with their secular
education.   ' At the time most important for their moral
and religious instruction, they were left without a chance

[1] *Hansard* 1836, XXXII, p. 273.

[2] *Bill to amend an Act*, 3 *and* 4 *Will. c.* 4, *for regulating the labour of
children :   Parl. Pap.* 1836, IV, 1.

[3] *Hansard* 1836, XXXIII, p. 738.

of improvement. During the week they had no time, and on Sundays they were too much exhausted to attend any school. He was a great friend to political reforms ', he went on to say, ' but political reforms should always be accompanied by the moral education of the people. If not, those reforms would be misused, and would be turned to evil.'[1] Though the Government carried their motion, it was by a majority of two only (178 to 176),[2] and realising that the opposition to this measure was widespread and strong, and being unwilling to court further unpopularity, they decided to drop the Bill.

Not only so, but vigorous administrative action to secure a stricter observance of the law was undertaken. New instructions were before long issued to the Factory Inspectors. The occasion for these was a letter of 16th June, 1836, addressed by the Board of Trade to the Home Department.[3] ' The President of this Board ', the letter stated, ' with the concurrence of the Home Office, intro-duced [in the spring of this year] into Parliament a Bill for the purpose of suspending the operation of the pro-gressive clauses relating to children between twelve and thirteen, which were to come into operation on the 1st March last. The opinion of the House of Commons upon that measure having been declared in a way which left

---

[1] *Ibid.*, p. 750. *Cf.* also Lord Ashley's description of the measure as one ' to legalise the slavery of some forty thousand children, for the most part females. A more faithless proposal was never made to the integrity and understanding of a legislature : the pledges of the country that children should be protected up to a certain point ; the compromise between the masters and the operatives—guaranteed by the interposition of the Government . . . were all equally violated.' From an article in the *Quarterly Review*, quoted in *Life and Work of Lord Shaftesbury.* Hodder.

[2] *Hansard* 1836, XXXIII, p. 788.

[3] *Directions to Factory Inspectors : Parl. Pap.* 1837, XXXI, pp. 123-5.

no hopes of its becoming law, the Bill was withdrawn, and assurance given to the House of Commons that . . . the Government . . . would use every endeavour to give [the law] full operation. . . . A point upon which their Lordships think the attention of the Inspectors and Sub-inspectors should be particularly directed is to the necessity of the Education Clauses being strictly enforced. Hitherto great indulgence has been shown with respect to this part of the Law, and, no doubt, serious inconvenience will attend its strict execution ; but their Lordships, after what has passed, do not consider themselves justified in allowing any further latitude upon the subject.' This was duly communicated to the Inspectors, Horner, Saunders, and Howell—the appointment of Rickards had recently been terminated—in a letter from the Home Department on 25th June, 1836. ' I am directed by Lord John Russell to draw your attention to the enclosed extract of a letter addressed to this Department by direction of the President of the Board of Trade, in consequence of the decision to which the House of Commons have come, on the Bill for amending the Factory Act, lately introduced by him. The reference which the President of the Board of Trade makes to the want of sufficient zeal of superintendence is, in Lord John Russell's opinion, mainly applicable to the District lately in charge of Mr Rickards, whose weak state of health necessarily rendered his services not so efficient as they might have been. . . . .' In the same month a new inspector was appointed in place of Rickards, but the important district of Lancashire and Yorkshire, for which the latter had been responsible, was now assigned to Leonard Horner, whose district (Scotland, northern counties, etc.) was taken over by the new inspector, James Stuart. Additional superintendents, acting under the direction of the inspectors, were appointed; and in October the inspectors were instructed to report to the Secretary of State quarterly in future, instead of half-yearly. Obviously the way was being cleared for a tightening up of the process of supervision.

The effects of the stricter administration soon began to be evident, with a consequent increase in the number of factories where some kind of education was given to the children under thirteen. Whereas factory schools had hitherto been the exception they now became more common, though far from general. At this period, for instance, Mr McConnell, ' one of the largest cotton spinners in Manchester ', opened a school on the factory premises. ' He is determined ', reported the district inspector, ' to have it on such a footing that the children shall receive an excellent education. In the Manchester paper I saw an advertisement, by Mr McConnell, for a schoolmaster and schoolmistress, offering very liberal terms. A committee of the adult operatives in the mill had been formed for the purpose of aiding Mr McConnell in carrying through his plan of his Factory school.'[1] Two years later the inspector was able to report that this school was easily the best in his district. ' They have provided a large, well-warmed and well-ventilated room, suitably and substantially furnished; they have engaged a competent and zealous master and mistress; reading, writing and arithmetic are taught to the children of both sexes; the girls are instructed in different kinds of needlework, and

[1] *Reports of Factory Inspectors : Parl. Pap.* 1837, XXXI, p. 63.

excellent maps are provided, and preparations are now making for teaching geography. Religious and moral training and habits of order, good breeding, and cleanliness and attention to neatness in dress have been objects of constant attention from the commencement. . . . The children are employed in the mill six hours a day and attend school three hours.'[1] Though a considerable number of mill owners in Horner's district still excluded all children under thirteen years, there was ' a great increase in the employment of children for short time in all parts '. The strong dislike to the Act which existed among a large number of the most reputable mill owners had greatly subsided, he reported in January 1837,[2] but the lack of proper schools and teachers still presented a great obstacle.

An account was given at this time of a test given by an inspector to the children of thirteen and fourteen years of age in a number of factories. Armed with a New Testament and a spelling book the inspector had the children brought before him, one by one, for examination. Of 2000 children examined :

186 did not know the alphabet.
372 knew the alphabet only.
509 knew words of one syllable only.

___

Making 1067 who could not read.
322 read the Testament with difficulty.
611 read it with ease.

___

2000

---

[1] *Reports of the Factory Inspectors on the Educational Provisions of the Factories Act :* Parl. Pap. 1839, XLII, p. 357.
[2] *Reports of Factory In pectors :* Parl. Pap. 1837, XXXI, p. 92.

The number of those who could sign their names amounted to only 441, viz. 341 out of 1040 boys, and 100 out of 960 girls.[1] On visiting a small mill in Preston, where a schoolroom had been prepared on the premises and a woman engaged to teach the children, of whom there were seventeen between the ages of nine and thirteen, the inspector asked the schoolmistress what state she had found the children in as to education ; to which she replied : ' We are but just begun : but, Sir, they are as ignorant as Hottentots ; only three could manage to read the Testament, and the greater number did not know their letters.'[2] At another mill in Bradford the inspector inquired of the schoolmaster what books he was using. ' Books, Sir,' he replied, ' why, I have had to put the greater number of them in the alphabet.' It was clear that the education given and required was of the most rudimentary kind.[3]

Greater vigour was now shown in prosecuting employers who did not comply with the Act. Whereas in the Manchester district during the period September 1834 to December 1835 there were only six convictions against employers for offences against the education clauses, and none at all in the Leeds and Huddersfield districts,[4] Horner reported that during the first three months he was in charge of these districts he had instituted 114 prosecutions, involving 90 for the offence of employing children without a certificate of school attendance.[5]

The small factory, employing too small a number of children to make the establishment of a school on the premises feasible, had for long been commented on by the

[1] *Ibid.*, p. 99.   [2] *Ibid.*, p. 62.   [3] *Ibid.*, p. 62.
[4] *Return of the Names of Persons fined under the Factory Acts : Parl. Pap.* 1836, XLV, pp. 171, *et seq.*
[5] *Reports of Factory Inspectors : Parl. Pap.* 1837, XXXI, p. 57.

inspectors as being the greatest difficulty. Either the mill owners were deterred from adopting the 'relay' system and from employing children, or the children attended any so-called school that might be casually accessible and in which the education was commonly of the most worthless kind.[1] In the hope that such employers might be induced to combine to maintain a single school, one of the inspectors circulated in September 1837 details of a scheme, suitable for adoption where several factories were situated within a moderate distance, under which this end might be achieved. He assumed for the purpose of his scheme that there were 300 children altogether in the neighbouring factories, 200 of whom would be in the mills and 100 in school at the same time. He estimated that the cost of erection and of furniture might be £300. This should be raised by shares of £10 each, a number of shares being assigned to each factory in proportion to the number of children usually employed, and the shares to be considered as attached to the building, so that, if sold or let, the factory school shares should go along with it. Interest at the rate of five per cent. per annum should be paid upon the capital out of the school fees. The pupils should be charged 3*d*. per week. And if an evening school were held in the same building from eight to nine o'clock for the young persons working twelve hours a day, £40 a year might be obtained from that source. Thus the annual revenue would be

	£
300 children at 3*d*. per week.............	195
From evening school...................	40
	£235

[1] *Reports of Factory Inspectors : Parl. Pap.* 1837-8, XXVIII, p. 86.

The expenses of the school were estimated as follows :

	£
Salary of master	80
,, ,, mistress	50
,, ,, assistant master..............	20
,, ,, assistant mistress.............	15
Fuel and light...........................	15
Books and stationery.....................	20
Interest on capital......................	15
Ground rent, repairs and contingencies ...	20
	£235

The schoolmaster should obtain from each mill belonging to the school proprietors a list of all the children who were bound by the Act to attend school. He should every Monday attend at the counting house of each mill to correct his list, by adding the names of the newcomers and striking off those who had left ; and, at the same time, to deliver his certificate of attendance for the preceding week. ' If such a school were seen in a manufacturing town ', wrote Horner, ' a neat plain building, with a broad tablet on its walls inscribed " Factory School ", it could not fail to give the inhabitants a higher idea of the advantages of factory employment ; many more would be induced to send their children to factories, when they saw that their moral improvement was a special object of attention, and thus the general character of factory labour would be raised. Many, too, of those who now send their children to the mills, when they found that they were receiving substantial good, would set a high value upon the school ; and in place of the indifference, which now prevails to so great an extent, we should find them acting in concert with the mill owner, and watching that their children attended regularly, and did not lose advantages which they could purchase at so cheap a rate.'[1]

There was no reason to think, however, that this particular scheme met with much success ; and for the most part the schools attended by the factory children provided little education worth the name. A leading, and candid, mill owner informed the ' Select Committee on the Education of the Poorer Classes ' that he thought the quality of the education given in schools under the Factories Act ' almost good for nothing '. The manufacturers made some arrangement with some neighbouring person, or employed some person in the works, who gave a certificate which freed the manufacturers from responsibility. ' It sometimes happens ', added Mr Henry Ashworth, ' that some lame, infirm old woman, who is unable to gain a livelihood by work, undertakes to become the teacher of children ; she teaches everybody's children ; what is usually termed a dame school ; those are willing always to make a bargain with the mill owner that they will undertake the teaching of the children. . . . If it is convenient that is the best way of doing it ; if not the master manufacturer must find some place attached to his works, or some cottage just by, where the thing is insisted upon in some way to avoid the penalty.'[2]

In the absence of schools where a satisfactory education was given, the inspectors were clearly handicapped in bringing pressure to bear on the owners. ' It is not at

---

[1] *Reports of Factory Inspectors : Parl. Pap.* 1837-38, XXVIII, p. 118.

[2] *Report from the Select Committee on Education of the Poorer Classes : Parl. Pap.* 1837-38, VII, p. 236.

all an unusual thing for us to have certificates presented to us subscribed by the teachers with his or her *mark* . . . In the last quarter I had a school voucher presented to me with a " mark ", and when I called on the schoolmaster to read it before me, he could not. It had been written out by the clerk of the factory, and the schoolmaster had been called to put his mark to it. I have had to reject the school vouchers of the fireman, the children having been schooled in the coal-hole (in one case I actually found them there), and having been made to say a lesson from books nearly as black as the fuel, in the intervals between his feeding and stirring the fire of the engine boiler.'[1] The inspectors were now pressing for an amendment of the law to enable the deficiencies of the education of the children to be removed.[2] A better system of education, a supply of proper and qualified masters, and some assistance and encouragement towards building schools were wanted. A further difficulty to which attention had been drawn in the inspectors' reports was that of ensuring that reliable certificates of age were rendered in respect of the employed children. The Act required that the certificate should be made on the authority of a surgeon and should testify that the child had the ordinary strength and appearance of nine years, ten years, etc , as the case might be. One of the inspectors, reporting in 1836,[3] remarked that he had been struck by

---

[1] *Reports from the Factory Inspectors on the Educational Provisions of the Factories Act : Parl. Pap.* 1839, XLII, p. 358. *Cf.* ' the notorious coal-hole seminaries improvised in contempt of the Factory Acts.' Dobbs, A. E., *Education and Social Movements* 1700-1850, p. 164.

[2] *Reports of Factory Inspectors : Parl. Pap.* 1837-38, XLV, p. 58, p. 63, *Parl. Pap.* 1839, XIX, p. 447.

[3] *Reports of Factory Inspectors : Parl. Pap.* 1837, XXXI, p. 56.

the diminutive size of many children who were working twelve hours a day and hence ought to have been at least twelve years of age. It was evident that there had been either the most culpable negligence on the part of the surgeons or that fraud had been extensively practised upon them by an older child having been presented to them under a false name and the certificate so obtained used by a younger child. Although, no doubt, the masters were often cognisant of the deception, ' the culpability is fully as chargeable upon the parents of the children ', remarked Horner ; ' they [the parents] will resort to any species of deception about their age in order to obtain the wages of twelve hours' work.'[1]

Towards the end of 1838 each of the four inspectors was required to make a report ' on the effects of the educational provisions of the Factory Act, as exemplified in not less than twelve of the schools situated in his district ,' and also the inspectors were required to make a joint report ' as to any modification of the existing educational provisions of the Factory Act, which may appear to them desirable.' These reports,[2] rendered in January 1839, throw much light on the extent to which the educational clauses of the Factory Act had been successful. The nature of the occupation, the locality of the mills, the interest shown by the mill-owners, the scale of wages paid—these and other factors all contributed to determine the amount and the usefulness of the education obtained by the factory children. One of the superintendents, having 500 mills under his supervision,

---

[1] *Reports of Factory Inspectors : Parl. Pap.* 1839, XIX, p. 447.

[2] *Reports from the Factory Inspectors on the Educational Provisions of the Factories Act : Parl. Pap.* 1839, XLII, p. 353.

in reporting to the inspector of the district,[1] said that he could not name a dozen schools where the education was systematically good and the mill-owner personally cognisant of the progress of the children. ' The engine-man, the slubber, the burler, the over-looker, the wife of any one of these, the small shopkeeper, or the next-door neighbour, with six or seven small children on the floor and in her lap, are by turns found teaching the young.' As proof of the incapacity of those who were thus employed as teachers, he quoted some of the certificates given by them.

' this to sertify that 1838 thomas Cordingley as attend martha insep school two hours per day January 6.'

' Sir. The reason P. Harrison left me I suppose to be his objection to pay my demands, as he left me in arrears. Elizth Northern has not and will not pay me a penny ever since she came to me ; her plea is that you stop it out of her wage.—If you please, Sir, If you please Fairplay's a Jewel.—E. Hinchliffe.'

' The above Named Children has Been twelve Hours in this School After the Manner of Scollers in the past week.—Mary Collins.'

' This his to Certify that Christina Walker Comes to my School one halfe of the week.—Hannah Hargreaves.' A facsimile of the handwriting would have been required to render these specimens complete, added the super-intendent. As an example of the real condition of the clothing districts near Leeds, the results of a test given to the 325 children under thirteen years employed in eighteen mills were quoted :

47 could not read

---

[1] *Ibid.*, pp. 411-4.

E

45 could read only the alphabet

108 could read in the *Primer*

74 could read the spelling-book

51 could read the Testament.

In another locality within a short distance from Leeds, the superintendent gave the same test in 49 mills employing 498 children between nine and thirteen years :

26 could not read a letter

71 could read only the alphabet

126 could read in the *Primer*

86 could read in the spelling-book

169 could read the Testament.

Though the proportion of those able to read was higher in this instance, it clearly justified the inspector's statement that ' a state of great mental neglect was everywhere general '.

Of the books found in the schools, the same superintendent remarked: ' In some instances, a few Testaments, *Reading Made Easy*, and spelling-books, and half defaced papers of the British and Foreign Society may be found ; in others these, in leaves huddled together in a pile, obliterated by oil and indigo, illegible, are the only scraps from whence the required education may be gleaned.'

Fortunately, it was possible for the inspectors to mention a few examples of more creditable efforts to promote the educational welfare of the children. In the school at Marshall's mill at Leeds, the proprietor of which had given evidence before the Factory Inquiry Commission of 1833, ' no expense is spared to cultivate every faculty of the mind to ensure the happiness of the individual.'[1] Out of 138 boys and 151 girls (under thirteen years) attending

[1] *Ibid.*, p. 414.

the school, 122 boys and 107 girls could read ' in the Bible
and Testament ' ; and ' several instances might be mentioned of children now employed only six hours a day,
whom the Act allows to work longer time, but, on account
of the rapid advances the children are making, the parents
will forego a little pecuniary benefit in favour of their
children's improvement.'[1] At the school provided at the
cotton spinning mill of Cooke, Hyde and Company,
Manchester, the children attended three hours a day ; and
as the proprietors thought it desirable to facilitate attendance by making the fee as small as possible, the children
paid 1d. per week only. ' The children are required to
appear with clean hands and faces and their hair combed ',
the schoolmistress stated. ' On entering the school they
put on a slip, or pinafore, which they purchase on their
first entrance ; all being required to adopt the same
pattern, both in make and colour. . . . In the morning
the school is opened with singing and prayer, suitable
for all sects, and closed with the same in the evening. . . .
The education is varied every alternate day ; one day
sewing, machining, knitting, with reading, spelling and
questioning ; on the other day writing and arithmetic.'[2]
(Only girls were employed at this mill.)

The following points were discussed in the joint report
made by the inspectors[3] : In the 20th clause of the Act, it
was enacted that the school might be chosen by the
parents or guardians of the child. Now, parents often
chose, not the best, but the cheapest, school ; and it
sometimes happened that on this ground they refused to
send their children to a good school at the factory, where
a moderate fee was charged, because they could get what

[1] *Ibid.*, p. 397.   [2] *Ibid.*, p. 361.   [3] *Ibid.*, pp. 424-6,

they called 'schooling' elsewhere at a cheaper rate. To meet such cases, as well as those where the mill-owner employed a totally unfit person as a teacher on his premises, and those cases also where the children were taught in an unhealthy place, the inspectors recommended that no certificate of school attendance should be valid that had been given by any teacher declared by them to be unfit to serve as such. The schools attended by factory children were often not open on Saturdays. Moreover, Saturday was a shorter working day than the rest of the days of the week for the older employees. The 21st clause, however, provided that the children should have attended school at least for six out of the seven days of the week. To give the children, therefore, a partial holiday on Saturdays, as well as to allow for the difficulties of making attendance at all on these days, the inspectors recommended that, whilst the weekly number of hours of school attendance should remain unaltered (viz. twelve), it should be sufficient if they were spread over five days, provided that at least two hours attendance a day were made. They thought it desirable, too, that the form of the certificate of school attendance should be given in a schedule to the Act, and that it should set forth not only the number of days and hours of attendance, but also the periods of the day when the children were at school. Several of the mill-owners had expressed a willingness to unite to support a school in a central position which might be used in common by the children employed in several neighbouring factories. To facilitate such arrangements the inspectors thought it would be helpful if it were enacted that it should be lawful for any number of persons to agree with each other for the establishment of a school for the use of the children employed in factories, and to make rules for the management and for defraying the charges thereof, and to insert in their agreement penalties for the breach of conditions stated.   Finally, they suggested ' that wherever it should appear to any inspector that a new or additional school is necessary or desirable, to enable the children employed in any factory to obtain the education required by this Act ', it should be lawful for the Lords Commissioners of Her Majesty's Treasury to appropriate such sum as might appear to them necessary for the building, enlarging, or otherwise establishing such school out of any money which might have been granted by Parliament for promoting education.

CHAPTER III

THE FACTORY ACT OF 1844

THE number of children benefiting by the provisions of the Factory Act at this time was but a small fraction of the juvenile employed population of the country. In England and Wales the total number in 1838 was upwards of 31,500, but deducting those who were employed in silk mills, there were only about 23,000 who were compelled by the Act to attend school for a part of at least six working days each week.[1] The number had fallen considerably during the past few years : whereas, in Horner's district, there had been early in 1835 about 22,000 children between the ages of nine and thirteen years, there were in 1839 little more than 10,000.[2]

The first attempt at amending legislation had already been made in 1838, early in which year a Bill had been introduced by the Government.[3] The Bill provided that in future the certificate of age was to be given by surgeons in a prescribed form, which should state not only that the child was of the ordinary size, strength and appearance of a boy [or girl] of nine, ten, etc., but that the surgeon

[1] *Return of Mills and Factories, and the number of Persons employed :* Parl. Pap. 1839, XLII, pp. 1 *et seq.*

[2] Appendix to the *First Report of the Select Committee on Mills and Factories :* Parl. Pap. 1840, X, p. 158.

[3] *Bill for Regulating the Employment of Children and Young Persons in Factories :* Parl. Pap. 1837-38, IV, p. 1.

believed this age to be true. On the form, too, the child's height, colour of the eyes, and colour of the hair were to be stated. In this way, it was hoped to reduce the possibility of careless certification and of the misuse of the certificate. As regards education, provisions of a radically different character from those of the Factory Act of 1833 were adumbrated. It was proposed to abandon the requirement of a certain number of hours weekly of attendance at school and in its place a clause was inserted to the effect that ' no child who is unable to read shall be employed after the expiration of twelve calendar months from the passing of the Act, except by licences as herein-after provided.' Further, whilst young persons (i.e. between thirteen and eighteen years) might be employed not more than twelve hours a day, or sixty-nine in any one week, these were to be reduced to nine hours a day, or forty-eight in the week, in the case of those who were unable to read. Also,

> ' one of Her Majesty's Principal Secretaries of State shall cause to be published, from time to time, an easy book for the use of children in factories ; and after the publication of any such book by authority no child shall be deemed able to read who is unable to read any part of any such book ; and no young person shall be deemed able to read who is unable to read the book of the New Testament.'

Even the qualification of ability to read to this extent was not to be absolutely obligatory in all cases. The inspectors were to be authorised to grant a licence allowing children and young persons who were unable to read to be employed in any factory of which the owner proved to the inspector, either by the establishment of a school or by the regulations he might make and the means he might take for enforcing attendance at school of the children and young persons, or by other evidence satisfactory to the inspector, that he was earnestly furthering the education of the children and young persons employed by him.

No suggestion on the lines of the new proposal had come from the inspectors. Indeed, the President of the Board of Trade said in a debate not long afterwards that the inspectors had been the first to criticise the measure.[1] But though the proposal appears to be retrograde in character, and was likely to be much more to the liking of the employers than the provisions of the 1833 Act, there were reformers of undoubted sincerity who were urging it on the Government. W. E. Hickson, one of the commissioners appointed to inquire into the condition of the handloom weavers, in a report written about this time, had referred with approval to the plans adopted by Cobden and his partner in their cotton-printing works at Sabden, where it had been a rule since 1st January, 1838, that no child could be employed ' who may not be able to read and write with tolerable correctness, and who may not also know something of accounts ' ; and he had suggested for consideration that the school clauses of the Factory Act (the provision of which, as regards short hours, he wished to see extended to factories of hand-loom weavers, silk mills, cotton-printing factories and indeed all factories in which power was employed) should be abandoned, and an educational qualification substituted for compulsory attendance at school.[2]

[1] *Hansard* 1838, XLIV, p. 400.

[2] *Report by Mr Hickson on the condition of the Hand-loom Weavers :* *Parl. Pap.* 1840, XXIV, pp. 691, 692.

This Bill, however, came to nothing. Though it was introduced early in the year, the Government repeatedly delayed its second reading ; and when on 22nd June, 1838, Lord Ashley challenged this inaction, he failed by a majority of eight votes to carry the House with him,[1] and the session ended without anything having been done.

Early in the following year (1839) another Bill[2] was brought in, in which were embodied most of the recommendations of the inspectors outlined in their recent special report.[3] Children employed under thirteen years should attend school twelve hours weekly, including at least two hours on each of five working days. No school certificate should be valid if given by a teacher declared by an inspector to be unfit for the purpose. Factory owners and others might agree with each other for the establishment of schools for the use of children employed in factories, and appropriate arrangements to make the agreement binding were to be legalised. A clause was added later providing against any child having to attend a school in which religious instruction contrary to the wishes of the parent was given. A form of school certificate was prescribed :

' I hereby certify that the undermentioned child [children] employed in the factory of   , situated   has [have] attended the School kept by me at   for the number of hours, and at the time on each day specified in the

---

[1] *Hansard* 1838, XLIII, p. 968.
[2] *Bill for regulating the employment of Children and Young Persons in Factories : Parl. Pap.* 1839, III, p. 467.
[3] *Cf. supra*, pp. 53-55.

columns opposite to his [her] name [names] during the
week ending on Saturday the   day of
one thousand eight hundred and   , and that the
causes of absence are true to the best of my belief.

' (Signed),

' Schoolmaster

' [Schoolmistress].'

The inspectors were to be empowered to appoint 'a sufficient
number of persons practising surgery or medicine to be
certifying surgeons' for the purpose of giving certificates
of age.   Where such certificates were given by a surgeon
other than a ' certifying surgeon ', the certificate must be
countersigned by a justice of the peace.   The form of the
certificate was prescribed.   No certificate should be valid
except at the factory for which it was originally granted.
This Bill, therefore, embodied most of the points which
the inspectors had for long been urging on the Government,
and the probability is that it would have passed through
Parliament successfully but for the opposition of Lord
Ashley to the non-inclusion of silk mills.   These had been
excluded from the Act of 1833 so far as the provisions
limiting the age of employment of children and providing
for the education of the latter went, and the new Bill
proposed to re-enact the existing state of affairs in silk
mills.   No limit as to age was provided for in the case of
silk mills, and children might be employed in them up
to ten hours a day.   In justification of the Government's
attitude, Poulett Thomson declared that ' it was absolutely
necessary in order to their attaining the proper degree of
skill that children should be admitted into silk mills at an
earlier period ' than was necessary in cotton factories.[1]

---

[1] *Hansard* 1839, XLVIII, p. 1071.

On 1st July, however, Lord Ashley carried, in the teeth
of Government opposition, a proposal to the effect that
silk and lace mills should be placed on the same footing
as cotton and woollen mills.[1] On 22nd July, on further
discussion taking place in committee, it was clear that
the Government would not acquiesce in this extension ;
and a few days later, Lord Ashley having indicated that
he intended to oppose the Bill if the extension to silk mills
was not retained, Lord John Russell, the Prime Minister,
announced his intention of withdrawing the Bill.[2] Thus
a further session of Parliament ended without any progress
having been made.

The inspectors continued to draw attention to the need
for a new Act which should give them effective powers.
In their periodical joint report of August 1839 they
expressed the view that the Bill which had just been
withdrawn would have proved highly advantageous, and
they hoped that early in the next session another Bill would
be brought forward.[3] In January, 1840, Saunders wrote
that most of the persons on whom he had pressed the need
for providing schools had declined to do anything until
the ' permanent enactments respecting this subject and
the labour of children and young persons shall be
ascertained and settled by a new Act.'[4]

On 3rd March, 1840, Lord Ashley moved a resolution in
the House of Commons for the appointment of a Select
Committee to inquire into the operation of the Factory
Act and to report their observations and opinion thereupon

[1] *Ibid.*, p. 1077.
[2] *Hansard* 1839, XLIX, p. 914.
[3] *Reports of Inspectors : Parl. Pap.* 1840, XXIII, p. 24.
[4] *Ibid.*, p. 42.

to the House. No opposition was made to this motion, which was accordingly carried.[1] Lord Ashley was himself appointed chairman of the Committee, which met regularly during the remainder of the session of 1840, examining the factory inspectors and superintendents, and also a number of mill-owners and operatives. So far as the inspectors were concerned, their evidence was largely a repetition of the views and arguments which they had often made in their periodical reports. The value of the Committee's work and reports perhaps lies chiefly in the greater publicity which was thus given to these points, and in the added authority which the Committee's support gave to them. Among the principal recommendations of the Committee were the following.[2]

Under the Act as it then stood, the eight hours a day for which children might be employed could be taken at any time of the fifteen hours between half-past five in the morning and half-past eight at night ; and in a great proportion of instances the children were in or about the factory the whole day thus affording many opportunities of their being employed illegally. It was thus the general opinion that the most effective way of securing the restriction on the labour of the children, and the opportunities of education intended, would be to restrict the employment to half the working day, divided by the dinner hour of the factory. The Committee accordingly recommended[3] that children under thirteen years of age should not be employed more than seven hours a day, nor more

[1] *Hansard* 1840, LII, p. 860.

[2] *Report from the Select Committee on the Act for the Regulation of Mills and Factories : Parl. Pap.* 1841, IX, p. 557.

[3] *Ibid.*, p. 568.

than forty-two hours in the week, and that those who had been employed before the dinner hour should not be employed again after that time, and vice versa.[1] This arrangement would ensure that greater use would be possible of the National schools and of the British and Foreign School Society's schools, which were normally not open before nine in the morning or after five at night. Since, as a rule, the best schools were not open on a Saturday, the Committee recommended that the obligatory attendance should be restricted to five days of the week, of not less than two and a half hours a day.[2] Certificates should not be valid if the attendance were made before seven in the morning or after seven in the evening. They were of opinion, too, that the inspectors should be given power to refuse the certificates of teachers on the ground of gross ignorance or immoral character, and also to object to schoolrooms that were obviously unfit to be used as a school.

As regards the responsibility for the provision of schools, however, the Committee had nothing to say. They

---

[1] *Cf.* 'In 1828, and from thence downwards—thus five years before the present Factory Acts were passed—I was as a medical practitioner in Leeds professionally engaged in the daily and nightly visitation of several factories. I was employed by the mill-owners and paid by them, to stand between them and the public with reference to the effect of labour on their workpeople, with power to enter their factories at all times by day and by night, and if I found their employment prejudicial to the children, to put them to half-time, or discharge them altogether. This was the origin of the half-time system.' Robert Baker in an address : ' The Physical Effects of Diminished Labour,' in *Transactions of the National Association for the Promotion of Social Science*, 1859, pp. 554-5. Robert Baker was appointed a Superintendent of Factories in 1834, and became an Inspector in 1858. He retired in 1877.

[2] *Report from the Select Committee : Parl. Pap.* 1841, IX, p. 576.

quoted the replies of two of the witnesses who were themselves proprietors of mills.[1] ' Schooling either belongs to
the parents or it belongs to the state ; it does not belong
to the employer, in my opinion : it is either a parental or
a national duty.'   ' There are situations in which it would
be very onerous and expensive for the mill-owner to provide
schooling to the extent which the population, or those
employed in his mill, might require.'   ' He had better pay
higher wages to older hands than incur the expense of
having children if he must undertake to educate them.'
As to this, however, the Committee did no more than
remark that they could devise no precise remedy.   ' It
might be dangerous, in many respects, to hold the
Government responsible for providing schools in such
cases ; and they [the Committee] can only express their
sincere and cordial hope, that the rapid progress of the
prevailing feeling in favour of a moral and religious
education of the operative classes will speedily come in
aid of the difficulty.'[2]

One of the inspectors, Saunders, whose reports, together
with those of Horner, had for long shown an ardent desire
for an improvement in the educational facilities afforded
to the factory children, had indeed put before the Committee proposals of a comprehensive character for meeting
the difficulty.   And since, in certain respects, they fore-
shadowed problems which were to stand in the way of
reform for many years to come, it is perhaps worth
referring to them in some detail.   It would, Saunders
informed the Committee, be a great injustice to throw
the whole expense of building schools upon the mill-owners ;
in fact, equitably, he thought they ought not to be called

[1] *Ibid.*, p. 575.   [2] *Ibid.*, p. 577.

on for any portion of it.[1] In view, however, of the lack of funds, it was advisable to encourage them to assist. Referring to the Bill of 1839, and expanding a recommendation made in the special joint report made by the inspectors earlier in that year,[2] he suggested the addition of the following provisions :[3]

'That whenever it shall appear to the Lords Commissioners of Her Majesty's Treasury [*or to the Secretary of State for the Home Department, or to the Education Committee*], on the report of the inspector of factories [*or a Government inspector of schools*], that a new school, or additional accommodation, is required for the education of children employed in factories, it shall be lawful for the Lords of the Treasury to grant such sum as may appear to them necessary for the building, enlarging, or otherwise establishing such a school.

[*The sum to be thus granted might be limited to half of what may be required for the purpose, especially if the next proposition be admitted.*]

'That [*in the cases above described*] it may be lawful for the Lords Commissioners of Her Majesty's Treasury to advance, on loan, to the owners and occupiers of mills, or other persons willing to aid in the building, enlarging, or otherwise establishing factory schools, such sum as their Lordships may deem reasonable and proper.

'[*Due provision might be made for securing repayment of the capital and interest of such loans within five or seven years and for limiting the amount so advanced*

---

[1] *Second Report from the Select Committee on the Act for the Regulation of Mills and Factories : Parl. Pap.* 1840, X, p. 218.

[2] *Cf. supra,* p. 54-55.

[3] *Second Report from the Select Committee : Parl. Pap.* 1840, X, p. 285.

to half the actual expense of building or enlarging a school.] '

As regarded the management of the schools to be so established, Saunders suggested the following arrangement.[1] The general management and control should be vested in a committee appointed by a majority of the subscribers, who should have control over the secular instruction given. Each child attending the schools should read, or have read to it daily, a portion of the Holy Bible. No child should in any case be required to learn any catechism, or other religious formulary, to which the parent or guardian might on religious grounds object : but in all other cases instruction in the Church Catechism and in the doctrines and principles of the Established Church should be given. No teacher should be appointed unless approved of by the bishop of the diocese. A copy of all books which the committee might propose to use, relative to religious instruction, should be transmitted to the bishop for his sanction and approval. Thus early was the shadow of religious dissension cast over the efforts towards the reform of the education of the factory children.

In connection with the extension of the Factory Act to other branches, the Select Committee presided over by Lord Ashley reported that, as regarded mills for the ' winding and throwing ' of silk, so many children were absolutely requisite that it would be extremely difficult to introduce the same regulations as in the case of cotton and other mills, and they therefore recommended that a separate measure should be introduced for this trade.[2]

---

[1] *Ibid.*, p. 285.

[2] *Report from the Select Committee on the Act for the Regulation of Mills and Factories : Parl. Pap.* 1841, IX, p. 592.

And though ' ample evidence respecting the cruel and unnatural employment of children ' in lace factories had been given, yet in view of the inconvenience that restriction would cause (' in consequence of the great amount of fixed capital involved in lace factories, it is often found necessary to work the machinery for long hours ', one employer is quoted as having said in justification of non-restriction), the Committee thought that here, too, different regulations from those applicable to cotton mills would be needed, and recommended that these should be included in a separate Bill ' hereinafter to be introduced '.[1]

Shortly after Lord Ashley's Committee had reported, two Bills were accordingly brought forward by the Government. On 26th March, 1841, a first reading was given to a new Factories Bill,[2] and four days later another Bill[3] to deal with silk factories was also read a first time. Lace factories were left aside for the time being. The new Factories Bill followed closely the recommendations of the Committee as regards the hours of employment of children (including half-day employment only), the hours of school attendance, the form of rendering school certificates, and the power of inspectors to refuse certificates from inefficient or unsuitable teachers and from schools conducted on unsuitable premises. The Silk Factories Bill, whilst prohibiting the employment of children under nine years (in this respect putting employment in silk mills on the same footing as that in cotton and woollen mills), proposed that no child under thirteen years should be employed for

[1] *Ibid.*, pp. 592-5.
[2] *Bill for Regulating the Employment of Children and Young Persons in Factories : Parl. Pap.* 1841, II, p. 425.
[3] *Bill for Regulating the Employment of Children and Young Persons in Silk Factories : Parl. Pap.* 1841, II, p. 459.

F

longer than 59 hours in any week, or more than ten hours in any day, and that employment should be between the hours of 8 a.m. and 7.30 p.m. (in winter) or between 6 a.m. and 5.30 p.m. (in summer). No child under thirteen years should, after 1st January, 1843, be employed unless able to read any part of the New Testament, ' and, in proof thereof, shall have received from some clergyman of the Established Church, or from some such minister, duly licensed, of any other religious persuasion . . . a certificate ' according to a prescribed form which should be kept by the factory owner ; and every child under thirteen years so employed should in December, 1843, and in the December of each succeeding year, be similarly examined and certified to show that he has made satisfactory progress in education since the date of the last preceding educational certificate. Finally, no young person under fourteen (i.e. of thirteen years of age) should be employed more than ten hours a day unless able to read fluently any part of the Holy Scriptures, to write a fair copy in large and small hand, and to understand the four first rules of simple arithmetic, in proof of which a certificate from a clergyman or minister must be obtained. Part-time education for children, therefore, was not to be extended to employment in silk mills.

It was now, however, near the end of the days of the Whig Government, which finally collapsed in June 1841. It was succeeded by a new Government under the leadership of Sir Robert Peel. In the meantime, the two Factories Bills had had no chance of getting beyond the first reading, and thus a third attempt at legislative reform had to be abandoned.

The factory inspectors continued their task of enlightening

the Government as to the actual state of affairs in respect of the education of the children concerned, and of directing attention to the modifications required. In a special report, written in February 1842,[1] Saunders made a plea for the immediate establishment of a few experimental ' Government Factory Schools '. Though in some few mills, where a large number of children were employed, the owners had occasionally incurred the expense of providing a school, yet in the vast majority of cases the owners had been appealed to without success. This, he thought, was sufficient answer to the objection that Government assistance would damp or destroy the exertions of private individuals. Moreover, the existing scheme by which Parliament provided funds for promoting education, viz. by aiding associations such as the National Society and the British and Foreign School Society to make grants towards the building of schools where private subscriptions raised locally were forthcoming, was useless so far as schools in factory districts were concerned ; for the places most requiring factory schools were those in which persons able to subscribe towards the erection of schools did not reside on account of " the nature of the works carried on and the degraded state and condition of the lower classes.'[2] He accordingly proposed, for the

[1] *Report of Mr R. J. Saunders upon the establishment of Schools in Factory Districts :* Parl. Pap. 1843, XXVII, p. 385.

[2] *Cf.* ' The general principle on which the Committee of Privy Council acts is to offer aid on certain specified conditions, and in proportion to the amount of local effort . . . What is its practical effect ? Obviously . . . to make the most liberal grants in aid of those places which are comparatively wealthy . . . As the real need of a district increases, in the same proportion Government assistance decreases.' Rev. Reginald Gurney, Clerical Secretary to the Church of England Education Society, in *Transactions of the National Association for the Promotion of Social Science,* 1859, p. 377. Of course, some factory owners did contribute towards

erection of Government Factory Schools, five places in the West Riding of Yorkshire in which there were no efficient schools in operation and where there were large numbers of factory children.   And since the fees to be paid by the children would prove insufficient to meet all the expenses, he urged that the Government should supply the necessary money ' for a limited period (say three years) . . . by which time it may fairly be expected that the experiment, if successful, will lead to some general legislative measure.' Saunders's report went on to propose, much on the lines of his evidence given before Lord Ashley's Committee in 1840,[1] the various rules concerning the religious instruction which should be given, the effect of which would be to place the control and supervision under the Established Church. ' The masters and mistresses of such schools shall be members of the Church of England ', his proposed rules stated, ' and no . . . teacher shall be appointed without the approval of the Archbishops of Canterbury and York, each for his own province : and any . . . teacher shall be removed, if the Privy Council Education Committee, or either of the Archbishops, with regard to his own province, should at any time withdraw his con-

---

the provision of public schools. *Cf.* ' The effect of the Factory Acts is practically to throw on the manufacturers the obligation in the last resort of supplying education for the children whom they employ . . . Unless there be a school already existing near the mill, the owner must himself provide one . . . I heard of more than one instance where a factory master, on the verge of spending money in setting up a small school for the single purpose of giving certificates to his short-timers, was induced to make a considerable donation to enable the clergyman to get a grant from the Privy Council to establish a national school for the general good.' Education Commission : *Reports of Assistant Commissioners (Report of J. S. Winder). Parl. Pap.* 1861, XXI, Pt. II, p. 211.

[1] *Cf. supra*, pp. 64, 66.

currence to such appointment.'[1] Perhaps it was the devotion to the interests of the Church of Sir James Graham, now Secretary of State for the Home Department, to whom the report was addressed, that led to the report being printed and presented to the House of Commons in August 1842.[2]

An interesting account of the kinds of school attended by the factory children was given about this time by Leonard Horner.[3] His inquiry, conducted between January and April 1843, included 6872 children, attending 603 schools. Of the latter, 117 were factory schools (i.e. schools situated within the factory, or schools adjoining the factory, which had been established by the factory owner), and were attended by 3,155 children. 367 were private schools, attended by 2,689 children : these schools were described as being in general ' small assemblages of children in cottages, brought together by indigent old men or old women, without any qualification for teaching.' 62 were national schools, attended by 596 children. 30 were public schools connected with the Established Church, but not schools of the National Society, attended by 214 children. 15 were ' British ' schools, eight Wesleyan schools, and four Roman Catholic schools, attended by 125, 54 and 39 children respectively. Of the 117 factory schools, 16, attended by 860 children, were good. In other factory schools, and in some of the private schools, some little education was imparted ; but in the majority of both there was a mere nominal compliance with the

---

[1] *Report of Mr R. J. Saunders : Parl Pap.* 1843, XXVII, p. 393.
[2] See *infra*, pp. 74-5 n. as to the influence of Saunders's views on subsequent attempts at passing new legislation.
[3] *Reports of Inspectors : Parl. Pap.* 1843, XXVII, p. 346.

law. 4,500 out of the 6,872 children were getting no education worth the name. Saunders, in his report for the quarter ended 30th June, 1843, mentioned one incident experienced in a school being visited by the mill-owner. The latter, ' greatly to his surprise, found the schoolmaster in a deep sleep amid the unrestrained turmoil and uproar of the school. He kindly awoke him ; but instead of the schoolmaster viewing it as an act of kindness, it appeared to be quite the reverse, for he at once remonstrated on the cruelty of such conduct.'[1] Again, one of the factory schools visited had for a teacher an old disabled soldier, who had been a comber but had been long unable to work at his trade owing to an injury to his thumb. The school-room in the mill was small and filthy. When visited, three of the children were actually working a winding machine which had lately been introduced ; one of the girls was washing the floor, and the remainder were on benches, some with an old tattered Testament on their knees, but most without any books at all.[2] In Saunders's district, the children were attending schools as follows :[3]

3,367 Factory Schools.

4,159 Private or " dame " Schools.

1,547 Church Schools.

243 Protestant Dissenting Schools.

———

9,316

The number of children affected by the Act had continued to decrease, partly, perhaps, owing to depression in trade having led to a reduction in the demand for child labour but partly also no doubt to the disinclination of employers

[1] *Ibid.*, p. 356.   [2] *Ibid.*, p. 356.   [3] *Ibid.*, p. 359.

to make the necessary arrangements for school attendance. Whereas in 1838, in Saunders's district, there were some 10,627 children employed in cotton, woollen, worsted and flax mills, in 1843 there were 8,754.[1] In the district of T. J. Howell, which stretched from the Mersey to Cornwall, the number had fallen from 2,400 in 1838 to 900 only in 1843.[2]

In this latter year, another attempt was made to pass legislation with the view of making the provisions of the Act of 1833 more effective. On 28th February, 1843, Lord Ashley moved that ' the best means of diffusing the benefits and blessings of a moral and religious education among the working classes' might be taken into serious consideration.[3] To this Sir James Graham, the Home Secretary, speaking for the Government,[4] said that he had decided to submit measures to meet the situation. The subject of the education of the people, he asserted, had been more neglected in this country than in any other civilised nation. In face of so great a neglect, it would not be possible to remedy the entire evil at once ; but he proposed to deal with two classes in the current session. The first would refer to the pauper children in the workhouses, and power would be given for parishes to unite for the formation of district schools and for the cost to be borne from the poor rate. As regards factory children, the imperfect manner in which their education had been provided for in the Act of 1833 had rendered the provisions almost nugatory. It was his intention, therefore, to propose that children between the ages of eight and thirteen years employed in factories should not

[1] *Ibid.*, p. 373.   [2] *Ibid.*, p. 341.
[3] *Hansard* 1843, LXVII, pp. 47-75   [4] *Ibid.*, pp. 75-91,

work more than six hours and a half a day ; that if they worked in the morning they should not work in the afternoon, and if in the afternoon they should not work in the morning ; that they should attend school for at least three hours a day. He proposed further that in factory districts where subscriptions towards the erection of schools aided by public grants might be inadequate, the inhabitants should be enabled to procure a loan from the Exchequer, to the extent of one-third of the cost of the building, repayment of which loan would be obtained out of the poor rates in a period of ten years. The support of the school would be provided by fees paid by the children, not exceeding 3*d*. per week, or more than one-twelfth of the child's wages, and the balance from the poor rate of the district. He proposed that the schools should be managed by trusts comprising seven persons. The officiating clergyman of the district should be one, and he should have the power to nominate two of the churchwardens for the year as trustees. The remaining four should be elected by the magistrates from among persons satisfying a property qualification, of whom two should be millowners. These trustees would have the duty of managing the school, and also the power of appointing the teachers subject to the approval of the bishop of the diocese as to their competency to give religious instruction to members of the Established Church.[1] The Holy Scriptures were to

---

[1] ' The fatal claim was made that in the new schools the headmaster should be a churchman, and although Sir James Graham has been much censured for that proposal, the following letter to Mr Kay Shuttleworth, seems to prove that Mr R. J. Saunders was the author of it. He was returning the clauses as then drafted, and wrote : " There is one most important omission in these regulations, which is that the master must be a member of the Church of England." ' Frank Smith, *Life and Work of Sir James Kay Shuttleworth* (1923), p. 142. *Cf.* also letter from Sir James

be taught daily, but no child would be required to receive instruction of the catechism of the Church of England or to attend the Established Church whose parents objected on religious grounds. The children of the parents belonging to the Church of England were to be instructed in the Catechism and Liturgy of the Church of England separately from the other children, and that daily. The schools were to be inspected by the clerical trustee.

The House appeared at first to be fairly satisfied with these proposals. Lord John Russell, speaking as leader of the Whig opposition, did refer incidentally to the religious aspect but apparently not in the expectation that it would prove a serious difficulty. ' If it could be shown that not one child of a dissenter need be excluded from these schools by the strictness of the rules imposed on them—that there would be no occasion for any parents to be alarmed for the religion of their children—then he should say that it would be far better to accept the regulations and not cavil at the parts of a scheme which

Graham to the Bishop of London, 27th December 1842 : ' Last spring I ventured to express a strong opinion that the law which now provides for the instruction of children employed in factories is most defective, and that the ignorance of large masses of the population congregated in these districts is disgraceful to the Government, and inconsistent with the peace of the country . . . You referred in terms of commendation to the opinion of Mr Saunders on this subject. I have carefully considered his reports ; I have had confidential communications with him ; I have directed him to confer with Mr Shuttleworth, the Clerk of the Council, and with Mr Horner, the Inspector General of Factories, and to endeavour to frame clauses not open to the objections urged to the former proposals, but such as the Church might reasonably concede, and the Dissenters adopt, as a scheme of compulsory scriptural education. I myself have had frequent conferences with these three gentlemen, and the result has been the preparation of the clauses which I now submit, in confidence, for your consideration.' Parker, C. S., *Life and Letters of Sir James Graham*, 1792-1861, vol I. (1907), pp. 342, 343.

they could not object to as a whole ' ; and he concluded
by trusting ' the Government would consider the question
still further, and that such larger and more matured
measures would be brought forward as would enable
Parliament hereafter to say that they had improved the
religious and moral, as well as the physical, condition of
the people.' The only discordant note was raised by
Mr Hawes, the Member for Lambeth. It struck him, he
said, that the clergyman would have the whole superintendence and regulation of the schools. Such a power
must inevitably be jealously watched. Would it not be
possible, he asked, to make the dissenting minister also
a member of the trust ?

The new Factories Bill[1] was formally introduced a few
days later, on the 7th March, 1843. It included within
its scope children employed in silk factories in addition
to those in factories and mills covered by the Act of 1833.[2]
But although there was a provision that any children in
the factory districts, whether employed in the factories
or not, should have the privilege of attending the schools
at a fee not exceeding 3*d*. a week, it hardly justified
Graham's assertion that the Bill would go far to establish
a national scheme of education. Cobden estimated that
not more than about 60,000 children would attend the
schools.[3] The Bill obtained a second reading on 24th
March, but already the opponents of Church control were
making their voices heard. Also, petitions ' numerous

---

[1] *Bill for regulating the Employment of Children and Young Persons
in Factories and for the better Education of Children in Factory Districts :
Parl. Pap.* 1843, II, p. 495.

[2] Sir James Graham stated that it was his intention to introduce a
separate Bill to include lace factories and print works.

[3] *Hansard* 1843, LXVII, p. 1470.

almost without parallel ',[1] poured in in protest. The
clause requiring the children to attend on Sundays in the
parish church the ' Divine service of the Church of England
as by law established ', except those whose parents should
notify their objection on religious grounds, gave particular
offence. Sir James Graham proposed some amendments,
in an endeavour to overcome the objections raised.[2] The
daily instruction in Church doctrines would be given in
a room apart from the school room, separate from the room
in which the children of dissenting parents received
instruction. During the time set aside for the Church
teaching, the dissenting children would receive instruction
in other subjects. On one day a week, three hours would
be allowed for religious instruction to dissenting children
by a minister of the chapel attended by their parents.
As regarded trustees, the clergyman, instead of having
the power to nominate two churchwardens, should
nominate only one person, the place of the second being
taken by a trustee elected by the subscribers and donors
to the school. The four remaining trustees should be
elected by ratepayers assessed at £10, no ratepayers voting
for more than two trustees. The headmaster, and he only,
should be subject to the veto of the bishop, the remaining
teachers being appointed by the trustees, subject to no
veto. Though these amending proposals were doubtless
sincerely meant to go some way to mitigate the situation,
it was soon clear that the passionate objection of the
dissenting parties would not thus be met. It was equally
clear that Sir James Graham would make no further
concession in regard to the predominance of the Established

---

[1] Sir James Graham, *Hansard* 1843, LXVIII, p. 1104.
[2] *Ibid.*, pp. 1108-1116.

Church in regard to religious teaching in the schools.
' I say that as a Minister of the Crown—that Crown being
the head of the Church established by law—I should
betray my duty if I made any concession on this point.'[1]
On 15th June he had to confess to the House that the
objections to his measure had not been removed or even
mitigated by the modifications he had proposed ; the
opposition had continued unabated ; and as the Government realised that it was essential to obtain general consent
and willing co-operation if the measure was to be operative,
he announced that they had decided to withdraw the
educational clauses. It was now late in the session, and
little time was left to remodel the Bill, which had therefore
to be dropped. A few days later a promise was given by
the Prime Minister that early in the next session another
Bill to amend the factory law would be introduced.

Had Graham's Bill been successful, it might well have
led in time to a general provision of schools in the industrial
districts ; and perhaps the passing of legislation for universal
compulsory education, which had to await another thirty
years, might have come about much earlier. ' Of all the
shortcomings of the nineteenth century,' Professor Fay
has written, ' the failure to provide national education
before 1870 was the most unnecessary. Adam Smith
advocated it a century earlier, and Scotland enjoyed it
two centuries earlier. But " religion ", as Graham said,
" the keystone of education, is in this country the bar
to its progress." '[2]

[1] *Hansard* 1843, p. 544.

[2] *Great Britain from Adam Smith to the Present Day.* Fay, C. R. (1928),
p. 355. ' To enter into the problem of education in the nineteenth century
was like entering among those rocks in India which are tenanted by many
millions of vigilant and irascible hornets.' *Peel and the Conservative
Party.* Clark, G. K. (1929), p. 345.

In the new Bill,[1] introduced by Sir James Graham early in 1844, no further attempt was made to aid the provision of schools. Though some controversy ensued in regard to the hours of employment of young persons, and a new Bill[2] had in consequence to be brought forward, the provisions concerning the employment and education of the children were passed virtually without opposition. The age at which a child might be employed was reduced from nine years to eight. The hours of employment between the ages of eight and thirteen years were limited to six and a half daily (in the case of silk mills the restriction was limited to children between the ages of eight and eleven years), and these must be either before the dinner hour or after that hour, but not both before and after. As regards the certificates of age, similar provisions to those of the abandoned Bill of 1839 were included.[3] In factories where young persons were restricted to ten hours a day, children also might be employed ten hours a day on three alternate days in the week, provided that they were not employed on the remaining days and provided also that they attended school for at least five hours on the remaining week-days (other than Saturday). Otherwise children must attend school for at least three hours daily, no attendance, however, being required on Saturday. The owner of every factory in which a child was employed must obtain weekly a certificate from a schoolmaster, according to a prescribed form, that the child had attended school, as required by the Act, during the preceding week.

[1] *Bill for regulating the Employment of Children, Young Persons, and Women in Factories* : *Parl Pap.* 1844, II, p. 149.

[2] *Bill to amend the Laws relating to Labour in Factories* : *Parl. Pap.* 1844, II, pp. 187, 223.

[3] *Cf. supra*, p. 59.

He must also pay to the schoolmaster a sum not exceeding
2*d*. per week to be deducted from the child's wages (with
an over-riding limit of one-twelfth of the child's wages).
The inspector would have power to disallow the certificates
of school attendance if he was of opinion that the schoolmaster was unfit to instruct children by reason of incapacity
to teach them to read and write, from gross ignorance, or
from his not having the books and materials necessary
to teach reading and writing, or because of immoral
conduct, or from continued neglect to fill up and sign the
certificates of school attendance required by the Act.[1]
The new provisions became effective on 1st October 1844.

The first reports on the working of the new Act were
encouraging in tone. The objects in restricting and
regulating the labour of children, was the observation of
one of the inspectors early in 1845, had unquestionably
been more generally and effectively attained than they
had ever been : the grosser cases of ' mock schooling '
were put an end to, and the power given to the inspectors
to annul certificates of schoolmasters had had a salutary
effect in causing the factory children to be sent to a better
kind of school ; the managers of National, British and other
schools were now induced to admit factory children
readily, whereas previously, when attendance lasted for
two hours only, the inconvenience and interruption caused
had often made then disinclined to do so.[2]

The depression in trade, which had begun about 1837
and had been severest about 1840 to 1842, was passing
away, and a greater demand for labour was manifest. The

---

[1] 7 Vict. c. 15.
[2] *Reports of Factory Inspectors : Parl. Pap.* 1845, XXV, pp. 243, 244,
262, 270.

7042 children employed in 1842 in Horner's district (chiefly in Lancashire) had increased to 14,441 in 1845, and to 16,349 in the following year.[1] Factories which had excluded children during the years following the passing of the Act of 1833 now began to employ them again. This was no doubt to be attributed, first to the restriction of the employment of the children to half a day and the consequent simplification from the employer's point of view of the regulations and the smaller likelihood of the law being infringed, and, secondly, to the fact that in at least some of the processes the source of supply of competent labour had been cut off by the exclusion of children.[2] In Saunders's district (chiefly in Yorkshire) the number of children employed in accordance with the Act rose to 16,538 in 1845, and to 20,389 five years later.[3] In 1855 Horner mentioned 21,554 as the number of children employed in his district, an increase of over five thousand during the preceding four years.[4] Indeed the number continued to rise steadily over the country until full-time attendance at school became compulsory in the seventies, as shown by the following table, which relates to the number of children employed in the United Kingdom :[5]

[1] *Reports of Factory Inspectors : Parl. Pap.* 1846, XX, pp. 567, 1114.

[2] *Ibid.*, p. 1114.

[3] *Reports of Factory Inspectors : Parl. Pap.* 1850, XXIII, p. 260.

[4] *Reports of Factory Inspectors : Parl. Pap.* 1856, XVIII, p. 229.

[5] *Reports of Factory Inspectors : Parl. Pap.* 1863, XVIII, pp. 501 *et seq.* 1868-69, XIV, p. 479.

	1838	1850	1856	1862	1868
Cotton factories	12,327	14,493	24,648	39,788	41,674
Woollen ,,	6,203	7,094	6,703	7,969	6,767
Worsted ,,	4,534	9,956	11,228	13,178	26,069
Flax ,,	1,767	1,581	1,856	3,539	4,672
Silk (8 to 11 years)	4,452	1, 498	1,686	1,832	764
	29,283	35,122	46,071	66,306	79,946

In 1846 Saunders made an interesting survey of the
schools in his district attended by the factory children.
These schools were classified into :

1. Schools conducted in a satisfactory manner.
2. Schools not conducted in a satisfactory manner, but
   in the management of which there was reasonable
   ground for expecting steady improvement.
3. Schools which could not be classed under either of
   the two first classes, but which were not so obviously
   inefficient as to justify the inspector in annulling
   the certificate of the teachers.
4. Schools, the certificates from which it was probable
   the inspector would have to declare invalid.

The result of the survey is shown in the following table :[1]

		State of Efficiency of School				Total
		1	2	3	4	
Public Schools	National or Church	46	31	7	2	86
	Dissenting	17	15	2	—	34
Factory Schools		5	6	13	5	29
Private or Dame Schools		14	56	85	33	188
		82	108	107	40	337

[1]*Reports of Factory Inspectors : Parl. Pap.* 1847, XV, 464.

Fifteen years later a similar inquiry was conducted in the district (which, however, had by that time been enlarged geographically). The substantial improvement in the educational standard of the schools, as shown by the classification, and the large increase in the number of public schools and the decrease in that of private schools are noteworthy features of the inquiry, the results of which are summarised in the following table :[1]

		State of Efficiency of School.				Total
		1	2	3	4	
Public Schools	National or Church	96	67	—	—	163
	Dissenting	40	22	—	—	62
Factory Schools		8	12	14	—	34
Private Schools		1	51	32	1	85
		145	152	46	1	344

The number of factory children attending the various types of school for half-time in this particular district (which included the West Riding of Yorkshire) at various times is shown in the table below :[2]

		1843	1846	1860
Public Schools	National or Church	1,547	4,434	11,611
	Dissenting	243	2,272	6,599
Factory Schools		3,367	3,038	5,046
Private Schools		4,159	6,037	3,617
		9,316	15,781	26,873

[1] *Reports of Factory Inspectors : Parl. Pap.* 1861, XXII, p. 410.
[2] *Reports of Factory Inspectors: Parl. Pap.* 1861, XXII, p. 408. In Horner's district (which included Lancashire) the number of children attending the different types of school in 1847 was: Public, 7,586: Factory, 3,746; Private, 3,908; total, 15,240. *Parl. Pap.* 1847, XV, p. 832.

In 1843 nearly one half of the children attended private or dame schools, the great majority of which afforded a far from satisfactory education. 'The utter incapacity of the teachers,' wrote one of the factory inspectors about these schools, 'the inter-mixture and often predominance of infants, collected there to eke out the miserable pittance of the teachers ; the scarcity of books ; the tattered and dirty condition of those they have, generally the Bible, desecrated by such a use of it ; the larger proportion of the children doing absolutely nothing for nine-tenths of the time they are under confinement, and evidently enduring all the pains of doing nothing ; the noise, the close and tainted atmosphere, altogether render a visit to such mock schools a most painful duty ; exacting feelings of deep regret that the legislature should year after year do so very little in proportion to what is wanted towards the effective measures for the removal of this most dangerous and crying evil.'[1]

The figures in the preceding table reflect, however, the considerable growth during the period under review of attendance at schools under the aegis of the Established Church, of the various nonconformist denominations, and of the (undenominational) British and Foreign School Society and, in general, provided with assistance from the Privy Council Education Committee.

The stipulation of the Committee of the Privy Council on Education that before making a grant in aid of the erection of a school a certain sum must be raised in the locality of the school often continued to operate hardly in the factory districts, where, frequently, few persons resided from whom contributions could be obtained.

[1]*Reports of Factory Inspectors : Parl. Pap.* 1851, XXIII, pp. 227, 228:

The efficiency, moreover, of these schools that were provided partly from public grants suffered by want of sufficient funds. Premises recently erected were sometimes saddled with debt, and efficient teachers were not forthcoming because of the trifling emoluments offered. ' Until very different opinions prevail as to the emoluments of schoolmasters and until a higher status be conceded to them, persons of talent and energy and commendable ambition will not enter the profession,' remarked Horner. ' At present schoolmasters are paid salaries that are less than the annual income of a bricklayer's labourer.'[1]

In 1851 an inquiry, somewhat similar to that carried out a few years earlier in the district of Saunders, into the kinds of schools attended was made in Horner's district. The 427 schools attended by the factory children were all visited by the inspector or by one of his five assistants. The distribution in respect to the category of the managing body or to ownership, together with the number of factory children attending are shown in the following table :[2]

Denomination of School	No. of Schools	No. of Factory and Print Works' Children Attending		
		Boys	Girls	Total
Church (including 105 National)	177	4,515	2,232	6,747
British and Foreign Society	28	1,346	518	1,864
Wesleyan	25	512	263	775
Independent	3	50	32	82
Baptists	3	59	22	81
Swedenborgian	3	123	48	171
Endowed Grammar Schools	10	153	45	198
Roman Catholic	8	171	38	209
Established by the owners of Factories	52	1,669	1,150	2,819
Private Schools	118	1,405	877	2,282
	427	10,003	5,225	15,228

[1] *Reports of Factory Inspectors : **Parl. Pap.** 1846, XX, p. 1115.*
[2] *Reports of Factory Inspectors : Parl. Pap. 1851, XXIII, pp. 297-303.*

As regards these schools, the results of the inquiry revealed the following state of affairs :

Church Schools.—With few exceptions the premises of these schools were found to be spacious, as judged by the standards of the time. 'Very frequently there are two rooms, and often small classrooms are attached to the principal rooms.' Only 70 of the teachers had been at training schools, and many of these for a very short time— a few months only. Of the schools, 41 were considered to justify the description excellent, with able teachers and 'the order and discipline good.' 74 were classed as of a second-rate order ; 47 very indifferent ; and 15 thoroughly bad—'little more than a mockery of education.' There were often 150 to 200 children under a single master, unassisted even by pupil teachers. The want of an adequate supply of books, maps and other materials for teaching was a very general complaint. In several schools the Bible and Testament were the only, and in many, the chief books used for teaching the children to read. Lending libraries for the use of the scholars were found in 45 schools.

British Schools.—Of the 28 schools, 15 were described as excellent, and 12 as of a second-rate order. One was extremely poor. 23 of the teachers had been to training schools. Pupil teachers were employed in 13 of the schools, the number varying from one to six ; but shortage of staff was common. Under a master and mistress, there were 253 children in one school, 226 in another and 200 in a third ; and in several other cases, the number of children was far in excess of the ability of even an able teacher to do justice to the children, at least without the assistance of pupil teachers. In all the schools the accommodation was found to be spacious, and in all instances there were two class-rooms. There was a lending library for the children in 11 schools.

Wesleyan Schools.—The classification excellent could not be given to more than four out of the 25 schools of this denomination. Ten ranked as second-rate, seven as very indifferent, and of four the reports were very unsatisfactory. Only six teachers in these schools had been to a training school. A total of nine pupil teachers were employed— divided among three of the schools. Four schools had a lending library.

Independent Schools.—One of these was second-rate, and the other two were very indifferent. There were no pupil teachers, and no lending library in any of the schools.

Baptist Schools.—One was second-rate and the other two very indifferent. None of the teachers had been to a training school : there were no pupil teachers, and no lending library.

Swedenborgian Schools.—One was excellent, and two second-rate. The teachers were untrained, and there were no pupil teachers. Lending libraries existed in two of the schools, ' but for the Sunday scholars only '.

Endowed Grammar Schools.—Three of the ten were excellent, five second-rate, and two very indifferent. Though in three instances the masters were ' well-educated men ' none had been to a training school. There were no lending libraries.

Roman Catholic Schools.—Of the eight, three were excellent, three were second-rate, and two very indifferent. One master had been to a Protestant training school, and in one school there was a pupil teacher. In three there was a lending library.

Factory Schools.—These were schools established by

the owners of factories for the children they employed, the schools being either on the factory premises or in the immediate neighbourhood. In some they were open to other children also. In general, the schoolrooms were commodious, but in some the children were not only crammed into very narrow spaces, but the rooms, from the noise of the adjoining machinery, were quite unfit for the purposes of a school. The schools were classified into—excellent, nine ; very fair, 19 ; moderately fair, two ; very indifferent, eleven ; very bad, eleven. In 15 schools only out of 52 had the teachers been to a training school. In five pupil teachers were employed. 17 schools contained a lending library.

Private Schools.—Of the 118 schools, there were only seven that could be called good ; 36 scarcely justified the description second-rate ; 39 were very indifferent ; and 35 were utterly worthless. At two only had the teachers been to a training school.

The inspector summed up the results of his inquiry in the following terms. ' Of the 427 schools, 76 only, that is, not so much as one-fifth, are good efficient schools ; 26 more are only tolerably good ; 146 are considerably inferior to these last, 112 are so low in quality that the term indifferent is better than they deserve. 66 are not only of no value but positively mischievous, as deceptions and a fraud upon the poor ignorant parents who pay the school fees. These are schools scattered over the whole of Lancashire, and a few of them in the four northern counties, and for all we know it is more than probable that if a similar inquiry were instituted into all schools for the humbler classes throughout the country the results would be very similar. Nothing, therefore, can be more fallacious than statistical tables giving the numbers of children attending schools, if these numbers be read as an indication that so many children are receiving education, that is, in any sound practical sense of that term.'

As proof, on the other hand, of the extent to which education could be given in a good school to factory children attending half the day only, attention was directed to the fact that in the 61 schools mentioned above in which pupil teachers were found, there were 28 instances of the pupil teachers having received their education while working half the day in the factory. That advantages were enjoyed and progress made by the factory children when they were able to attend a good school may also be gathered from an account of the ' British ' school at Lees, near Oldham, described at the time by H.M. Inspector of Schools for the district as without exception one of the most vigorous and stimulating schools which he had yet met with. ' The factory boys are among my best scholars,' the master of this school wrote to the factory inspector. ' Three or four, who have just left the school, being 13, and entitled to work full-time, had gone through the arithmetic three times, and were able to give solutions of the most difficult questions. Two others had not only worked through the arithmetic several times, but had also gone through Bridges' algebra three times before they were 13 years of age. Their knowledge of geography, grammar, and the other branches taught in the school was very good. I could add much to show the healthy state of education among the half-timers.'[1] A further picture of the work of the factory children attending this school was given a few years later (1858) :[2]

---

[1] *Reports of Factory Inspectors : Parl. Pap.* 1851, XXIII, p. 306.
[2] *Reports of Factory Inspectors : Parl. Pap.* 1857-8, XXIV, pp. 235-7.

Class	No. of Factory Children.			Branches of Learning in Each Class
	Boys	Girls	Total	
1	26	4	30	Reading, spelling, writing from copies and dictation, geography, history, grammar, including analysis of sentences, drawing, arithmetic.
2	17	8	25	Ditto, except drawing.
3	13	11	24	Ditto, except drawing.
4	19	8	27	Ditto, except drawing, and analysis of sentences.
5	13	6	19	Reading, writing and geography, arithmetic.
6	12	11	23	Ditto
7	10	9	19	Ditto
8	2	1	3	Ditto

The progress of the scholars was shown in greater detail in a further table :

	Boys	Girls	Total
No. reading in books of general information	88	37	125
,, ,, easy Bible narratives	22	20	42
,, ,, monosyllables	2	1	3
No. writing in copy books	110	57	167
,, ,, on slates	2	1	3
,, ,, from dictation	75	31	106
No. learning grammar	75	31	106
,, ,, geography	112	58	170
,, ,, history	75	31	106
,, ,, drawing of maps and objects	20	4	24
,, ,, analysis of English language	56	23	79
No. doing simple rules	22	21	43
,, ,, compound rules and reduction	39	28	67
,, ,, practice and higher rules	25	6	31
,, ,, mensuration	26	3	29
,, ,, mental arithmetic	112	58	170

Of the ten pupil teachers engaged in this school, six were half-timers previous to their apprenticeship ; and of five who had completed their apprenticeship as pupil teachers, three had been half-timers.

Further light on the amount of instruction received by factory children who were half-day scholars, and of their progress in comparison with children attending school whole time is given in the results of an inquiry made in 1853 by Alexander Redgrave (who had recently succeeded Saunders on the latter's retirement). The inquiry covered 135 'public' schools, 10 factory schools, and 39 private schools.[1] As regards the duration of school life, it was found that the children employed in factories were not withdrawn from school at a much earlier age than the ordinary children.

Period children had been in attendance	Factory Children			Children not employed in factories		
	Boys	Girls	Total	Boys	Girls	Total
6 months and under	2,648	2,853	5,501	3,004	2,057	5,061
1 year	1,939	1,618	3,557	2,315	1,305	3,620
2 years	1,169	972	2,141	1,612	887	2,499
Above 2 years	2,018	1,488	3,506	2,625	1,320	3,945
	7,774	6,931	14,705	9,556	5,569	15,125

The percentage of children at each of the periods of attendance shown approximated fairly closely in the two classes—factory and non-factory children. Yet despite the fact that the factory children were generally the lowest grade socially in the school—being sent to school only because their parents could not otherwise receive wages from them—it might be inferred that the desire of obtaining wage-earning employment operated as powerfully with the

[1] *Reports of Factory Inspectors :* Parl. Pap. 1852-3, XL, pp. 577-581,

parents in a somewhat better position as with the poorer parents of the factory children. The factory children included, of course, none under the age of eight years, whereas nearly 50 per cent. of the non-factory children in these schools were under this age. This needs to be borne in mind in considering the next table.

Course of Instruction	Factory Children			Children not employed in factories		
	Boys	Girls	Total	Boys	Girls	Total
Learning reading only	659	907	1,566	2,289	1,710	3,999
,, reading and writing only	1,353	1,789	3,139	1,865	1,297	3,162
,, reading, writing and four simple rules of arithmetic only	3,297	2,839	6,136	2,507	1,382	3,889
,, grammar, geography, history and the higher rules of arithmetic	2,465	1,399	3,864	2,895	1,180	4,075
	7,774	6,931	14,705	9,556	5,569	15,125

Unless allowance were made for the under-eight children among the whole-time scholars, the table would give the impression that the factory children did much better than the latter. In order to make a closer comparison, figures which excluded the children under eight were obtained, and it emerged that 32 per cent. of the factory children were not sufficiently advanced to be taught the rudiments of arithmetic, whereas all the whole-time scholars over eight years of age had reached this stage. Factory children, it was clear, commonly entered the schools without having had any previous education, and but for

Course of Instruction	Percentage of Children (under eight excluded)	
	Employed in factories	Not employed in factories
Learning reading only	10.7	—
,, reading and writing only	21.3	—
,, reading, writing and four simple rules of arithmetic only	41.7	48.9
,, grammar, geography, history and the higher rules of arithmetic	26.3	51.1

the Factory Act would probably have continued to grow up without attending school at all.[1]

Course of Instruction	No. of Children			Per-centage
	Boys	Girls	Total	
Learning reading only	—	20	20	1.2
,, reading and writing only	34	146	180	11.0
,, reading, writing and four simple rules of arithmetic only	392	372	764	47.0
,, grammar, geography, history and the higher rules of arithmetic	334	329	663	40.8
	760	867	1,627	100.0

There were, however, in the particular district concerned in this inquiry, five schools established by factory owners

---

[1] *Cf.* ' I noticed a general superiority in the day scholars over the half-timers, when a fair comparison could be made between them. Take, by way of illustration, the following analysis of the classes of the Rochdale

who took an especial interest in them, of which particulars are given in the table immediately preceding. In one instance children were not permitted to be employed unless having previously been in attendance at the school for a certain period ; in the others preference in being given employment was extended to the children whose attendance at the school was most regular. As the duration of attendance of the children at these five schools was not very different from that in the schools generally covered by the inquiry, the much greater progress made by the children might be attributed to the requirement that some amount of attendance should be made before employment began, to regularity of attendance, and to the general stimulating

school, one of about 40 which I made. All the children after half-time age are omitted, and H and D stand for half-timers and day scholars respectively :

| Classes | Age of Scholars | | | | | | | | | | | | Total | |
| | 8 | | 9 | | 10 | | 11 | | 12 | | 13 | | | |
	D	H	D	H	D	H	D	H	D	H	D	H	D	R
I	1	–	2	–	13	3	20	6	15	17	6	4	57	30
II	1	–	9	2	11	6	7	7	6	12	3	2	37	29
III	5	9	8	1	13	1	7	11	2	11	–	1	35	25
IV	7	–	9	2	8	10	2	15	–	6	1	1	27	34
V	16	1	8	2	7	14	–	14	1	18	–	–	32	49
VI	22	4	11	10	–	14	1	16	1	12	–	1	35	57
VII	13	1	3	8	3	11	–	5	–	3	–	–	19	28
VIII	6	3	1	9	–	11	–	10	–	5	–	1	7	39
Total	71	9	51	34	55	70	37	84	25	84	10	10	249	291

After making all allowances for the disadvantages under which half-timers labour, the superiority of the day scholars, which an inspection of the table will at once show, is too marked to be accounted for, except on the supposition that the mode of their instruction is more effective.'
Education Commission : *Reports of Assistant Commissioners (Report of J. S. Winder) : Parl. Pap.* 1861, XXI, Pt. II, p. 232.

effect of the personal interest and support of the employers.[1] Unfortunately there appeared to be few of the latter of whom so favourable an account could be given.

Robert Baker (who succeeded Horner on the latter's retirement in 1858) found from an extensive investigation in 1861 that on the average ' half-timers ' were older than the ordinary day scholars attending the same schools as shown in the table below :[2]

	Boys		Girls	
	Years	Months	Years	Months
First Class	0	8	1	3
Second Class	1	0	1	3
Third Class	1	2	2	0
Fourth Class	2	2	3	3

The difference between ages and attainments diminished as the attendance at school increased ; and this was doubtless due partly to the greater regularity of attendance of the factory children. ' In respect to those children between the ages of eight and thirteen, who are employed in factories and attend school for three hours daily during five days in the week,' one of H.M. Inspectors of Schools

[1] *Reports of Factory Inspectors : Parl. Pap.* 1852-3, XL, p. 583.

[2] *Reports of Factory Inspectors : Parl. Pap.* 1862, XXII, p. 260. *Cf.* also, ' There can be no doubt that the half-timers in general are at school at a later age than the day scholars ; in fact, they nearly all remain until 13, the practical limit of school life ; but it by no means follows that the total length of time during which they have at school is proportionately later. I satisfied myself, by repeated questions to individual children, and by an inspection of school registers, both at Rochdale and Bradford, that on the average, half-time children, at the commencement of their work, have been a much shorter time previously at school than day scholars of the same age.' Education Commission : *Reports of Assistant Commissioners (J. S. Winder) : Parl. Pap.* 1861, XXI, Pt. II, p. 229.

in Lancashire had written to Horner some years earlier,[1] ' I am happy to assure you that my impression is that they are equal in intelligence and attainments, on the whole, to any class of children attending the schools I inspect. The question naturally occurs, how is it that children who attend school for three hours a day only are equal in attainments to those who are able to attend for six hours a day. I answer that the *regularity* of their attendance compensates for the fewer hours. The attendance of the children of the labouring classes at our national schools is very irregular. The half-timer is never absent on a school day ; he keeps adding line upon line ; and he is not allowed time to forget his last lesson.' The writer, however, added in a postscript to his letter that of course he was referring only to those half-timers who had been at the schools for a considerable time. There were others, he observed, who came to school for the first time at an advanced age, and were to be found in the lowest class.

' Three-fourths of the " half-timers " cannot read when they are admitted ', a correspondent from a Cheshire school wrote in 1861.[2] ' Should they be so fortunate as to remain at the mill a sufficient length of time, and to have parents who are willing to provide them with books, their progress is very satisfactory, especially in the lower classes. There are, however, constant changes taking place, and many parents are totally indifferent about their children's progress, which renders it impossible for " half-timers ", as a general rule, to get into the first class. When a " half-timer " is ready to pass into a high class, it not infrequently happens that the boy's parents, before they

---

[1] *Reports of Factory Inspectors : Parl. Pap.* 1852-3, XL, pp. 545-547.
[2] *Reports of Factory Inspectors : Parl. Pap.* 1862, XXII, p. 254.

will provide him with a new book, will take him away from
the mill for a time, and then send him back again, in the
hope that the old book will be sufficient. Should he,
whilst working at other mills, attend a factory school
where they deem his old reading book sufficient, it is very
probable we may not see him again. We have this week
admitted four " half-timers " ; out of the four, three
are over twelve years of age, and are not able to distinguish
one letter from another.

' These mill children in the lower classes generally,' the
writer continued, ' are not deficient in intelligence, but,
owing to the neglect and carelessness of parents, have
never attended either day school or Sunday school before
they are sent to work. Those in the upper classes were
scholars at this school before they went to work. Most
of the children attend school in the afternoon. I think
if they could come part of their time in the morning, say
for a month at once, and change, they would have a better
chance to improve, as they are tired and weary when
they come to school in the afternoon. Where this is done
it acts well.'

Surveying a large number of first-hand accounts, of
which the preceding is but a specimen, Baker drew some
broad general conclusions.[1] (1) Notwithstanding that
by 1861 there had been a wide extension of ' public '
schools, there were still large numbers of children who
never attended a school before entering into employment.
(2) These children were for the most part the children of
negligent or improvident parents, or orphans, or otherwise
destitute. (3) Two-thirds at least of the ' half-timers '
appeared not to be sent to the school previous to being

[1] *Reports of Factory Inspectors : Parl. Pap.* 1862, XXII, pp. 257, 258.

employed, and but for the Factory Act, the number of children receiving no education must be substantially increased. (4) Where 'half-timers' had attended school before being sent to work, they made nearly equal progress with whole-day scholars ; but where they had not been so sent, equality of progress was only the result of a higher average age over the day scholars.[1] (5) Where 'half-timers' attended school only in the afternoon, they did not make the same progress as those who attended in the morning, or in the morning and afternoon alternately. Baker urged the advantages there would be in requiring from all children a certificate of a certain minimum amount of education having been attained previous to employment ; and also a similar certificate in the case of those who had reached the age of thirteen, in default of which the education begun during the period of half-time employment should be carried on in a night school to an age not exceeding sixteen years until the required amount of education might be attained.[2] Proposals of a similar kind had indeed from time to time for some years past been suggested by the inspectors. 'If employment were made the reward of education ', Redgrave wrote in 1852, ' if a certain amount of acquired knowledge, or a certain number of years' attendance at school, were made the qualification for labour, an interest would at once be created in the right direction, the value of education would

[1] *Cf.* ' The schoolmasters who have had experience of both plans are unanimous in saying that half-time teaching is far more nearly equal to full-time than would be supposed. Some go so far as to assert that it is " very nearly as good ". All admit that a double school-time produces nothing like a double result.' Education Commission : *Reports of Assistan Commissioners (J. S. Winder's Report) : Parl. Pap.* 1861, XXI, Pt. II, p. 232.

[2] *Reports of Factory Inspectors : Parl. Pap.* 1862, XXII, p. 259.

be appreciated by those who are now insensible to it ; the punctual attendance at school, and the advancement of the child would then be the objects of the parents' solicitude.'[1] And in 1859 the factory inspectors, in a joint report, mentioned with commendation some instances of mill-owners having recently given a preference to the employment of young persons who were able to read. This had greatly promoted the interests of education in the neighbourhood. Until there had been generations who had themselves been educated, they remarked, it could not be expected that those who had had no experience of its advantages, would take any pains to send their children to school unless stimulated by some prospect of direct profit from their employment, attainable only by that condition. But any obligation of this sort, they added, should, of course, apply to all employments.[2]

During March and April of 1859 Baker caused an examination in reading to be given, by the certifying surgeons for age certificates, to 2,500 young persons between the ages of thirteen and sixteen offering themselves for employment in certain places. 42 per cent. were found to be unable to read at all. Baker himself examined eleven boys between the same ages in a Leicestershire cotton factory, being all the boys in that factory, and found that only two of them knew the alphabet. That there was a lamentable indifference on the part of many of the parents to the education of their children was already known ; but as several of the young persons concerned in the examinations referred to had doubtless already spent some time in the factories as children, Baker

---

[1] *Reports of Factory Inspectors : Parl. Pap.* 1852-3, XL, p. 516.
[2] *Reports of Factory Inspectors : Parl. Pap.* 1859, XIV, Sess. 2, p. 403.

H

concluded that there was a clear necessity for continuing at night schools the education begun before the age of thirteen years. In making the inquiry Baker had had in view the possible effects on industry of an educational test as a condition of employment being immediately made compulsory by legislation. Whilst the results served to indicate that it was too early yet for such a step, he considered that a prospective educational test, say, in five years, would be practicable. It had been found in the neighbourhoods where the surgeons had examined the young persons concerned, that there had been ' an impulsive rush to school ', under an impression that in future only those who could read and write would be employed. Baker was even doubtful whether, if legislation on the lines suggested were passed, the schools existing at that time would be sufficient to accommodate all the would-be pupils.[1] A somewhat similar experiment was carried out in the same year (1859) by the certifying surgeon in Leeds. During a period of six months, he examined 499 children between the ages of thirteen and sixteen years, and found that 123 only, or 24 per cent., could read. Of the 123, only 26 had been previously in half-time employment, the remainder having gained their education independently of factory legislation. Of the 376 young persons who could not read, 89 had been employed half-time in factories, attending school, while they were between the ages of eight and thirteen years, for various periods. But whilst these periods of half-time attendance at school were in some cases of considerable duration, yet, Redgrave commented, the number of children who were retained in

[1] *Reports of Factory Inspectors : Parl. Pap.* 1859, Sess. 2, XIV, pp. 439, 440.

factory employment up to the age of thirteen years was much affected by the great demand for the services of children of twelve years, and frequently less than twelve, in the numerous occupations wherein there were no restrictions.[1]

It had been one of the provisions of the Factory Act of 1844 that the penalties imposed on employers and others for offences under the Act should be applied by the Inspector, under the direction of the Secretary of State, ' in such manner as shall appear best for the education of children employed in factories '. The reports of the Inspectors occasionally throw some light on how the money was dealt with. In 1850, Horner reported that during the preceding six years since the passing of the Act he had distributed £1,738 in his district amongst 125 different schools.[2] He was especially concerned to give every encouragement to the formation of school lending libraries, for, he said, there were few things more likely to make the school itself attractive to the more advanced children and ' to make every fireside a school '. Some idea of the manner and objects of the distribution of the ' Penalties Fund ' may be gained from the following list of the actual distributions made in Horner's district during one half-year[3] :—

	£
" To the Church School at Clayton-le-Moors, for the establishment of a school lending library . . .	10
To St George's Church School, Chorley, for the like purpose	5

[1] Reports of Factory Inspectors : Parl. Pap. 1859, Sess. 2, XIV, pp. 443, 444

[2] Reports of Factory Inspectors : Parl. Pap. 1851, XXIII, p. 227.

[3] Reports of Factory Inspectors : Parl. Pap. 1852-3, XL, pp. 544-5.

£

To the Church School at Tunstead, near Bacup, for the purpose of obtaining a supply of school books and other materials for teaching. 10

To the National School for Over Darwin, near Blackburn, for the like purpose 10

To the National School at Great Marsden, near Burnley, for the like purpose, and towards the formation of a school lending library 10

To the National School at Waterside, Colne, for the like purpose 10

To Trinity Church School, Bolton, for the purpose of obtaining a fresh supply of books and other materials for teaching. 10

To the British School in Padiham, near Burnley, for the like purpose 5

To the British School in Sedberg, for the like purpose . 3

To the Church School at Buersil, near Rochdale, for the establishment of a school lending library . . 10

To the Day School attached to the Mechanics' Institute, near Newchurch, in Rossendale, for the purpose of obtaining a supply of books, maps and other materials for teaching, and towards the establishment of a school lending library for the use of the day scholars 10

To the National School of St Paul's, in Burnley, for the purpose of obtaining a supply of school books and other materials for teaching for the use of the day scholars 5

To the National School of St Peter's, in Oldham, for the purpose of obtaining a supply of books, maps and other materials for teaching, and towards the formation of a school lending library 20

To the National School of Littleboro', near Colne, for the like purpose 10

To the National School of Christchurch, near Preston, for the like purpose 10

To the British School attached to the Mechanics' Institute in Bacup, for the purchase of some school furniture, for the purpose of obtaining a supply of books, maps, and other materials for teaching and towards the improvement of the school lending library 20

To a newly established British School at Rough Lee, near Burnley, to obtain a supply of books, maps, and other materials for teaching 10

	£
To the National School of St Paul's in Preston, for the purpose of adding to the school lending library established by a former grant	5
To the National School of St Thomas, in Preston, to commence the formation of a school lending library.	5
To the School attached to the Roman Catholic Chapel of St Ignatius, in Preston, to procure the supply of books, maps, and other materials for teaching .	10
	198 "

Strange as it might seem, reported Horner in 1854, school books were one of the most common wants he was asked to supply, whilst ' in the better schools, the means of procuring maps have been thankfully received. Geography, when sensibly taught ', he added, ' when, instead of long wearisome lists of names of places, and latitudes and longitudes, physical geography is made the basis of instruction, it is always found a source of attraction and amusement to the children. To add to these, I have given a large terrestrial globe to some schools, and contemplate sending them to others. . . . Many excellent school lending libraries, consisting of books that are attractive to young minds, have been established by aid of this fund.' He had also endeavoured to assist the efforts of teachers by sending them copies of works dealing with education and the management of schools ; and these, he believed, had been found useful not only to the masters and mistresses but also to the pupil teachers, ' that invaluable work of the Committee of Council on Education, the greatest boon perhaps they have as yet conferred on the cause of education.'[1]

[1] *Reports of Factory Inspectors : Parl. Pap.* 1854, XIX, p. 378. See also *Communications from Edwin Chadwick, Esq., C.B., respecting the Half-time School System : Parl. Pap.* 1862, XLIII, p. 3.

The cotton famine of 1861-63 led to widespread unemployment. In 1862, half the total number of operatives in Lancashire were unemployed, and the great majority of the remainder were working short time. As part of the measures taken by the mill-owners to relieve distress, it was reported that the fees of factory children attending school were in some cases paid by their employers ; in others, classes of instruction for young persons were opened ; sewing classes were established for young women, ' who receive instruction in reading, writing and arithmetic in the morning and sewing and knitting in the afternoon.' At Blackburn, ' reading and industrial classes for men were opened. . . . Five days' attendance is exacted from men, for which they receive 2/-. They are educated in reading writing and arithmetic. They are also initiated into the mysteries of carpentry, tailoring, and shoemaking ; and the routine of these duties is occasionally varied by half an hour's drill.'[1] Redgrave, reporting in 1863, noted a slight reduction in the number of factory children attending school, caused chiefly by the withdrawal of the relief by payment of school fees from the children of parents who

---

[1] *Reports of Factory Inspectors : Parl. Pap.* 1863, XVIII, p. 455 *et seq.* *Cf.* also : ' It was only last week that one of the largest employers in Manchester, speaking of the patience and fortitude with which a population of many hundreds of thousands of operatives are now enduring an unprecedented amount of privation, said to me : " I know nothing in the range of my experience more remarkable than the development of the Lancashire character in the last fifteen years " ; and he ascribed it chiefly to the beneficent operation of the factory laws, adopted as they have been by the master manufacturers as their truest interests.' Rev. J. P. Norris, H.M. Inspector of Schools, in *Transactions of the National Association for the Promotion of Social Science,* 1862, p. 278. *Cf.* also, *History of the Distress in Blackburn* 1861-5, Gourlay, W. (1865) ; *History of the Cotton Famine,* Arnold, R. D. (1865) ; *The Facts of the Cotton Famine,* Watts, J. (1866).

obtained employment.[1] ' Where the income of the schoolmasters depended on the children's pence,' Redgrave
observed, ' the pressure has undoubtedly been felt by a
most discerning body of men who have throughout the
whole of the crisis worked energetically and under very
trying circumstances, and yet I find that they received
into, and continued in their schools many children who
were unable to pay their school fees, and in some instances
provided books, etc., so that the children should not suffer
from their inability to purchase them, and I have not heard
of a single instance of a school having been closed, or of a
schoolmaster having thrown up his office from the pressure
of the Cotton crisis.   There was a predominant feeling that
the children should be kept in school if possible, and all
heartily joined in working to this end.'   The following
statement by the Relief Committee at Bolton, a district
which was less affected by the famine than any other in the
county, is of interest :—' For children under 12 years of age
whose parents were receiving relief, and who could not
otherwise have been sent to school, the Committee arranged
to pay the school pence.   The highest number in attendance
has been 1045, the lowest 590, the average being 774.
The Committee have recently resolved that all children
from 12 to 16 years of age shall, while they remain unemployed, attend some school, and have agreed to pay their
school pence also.   The total cost of the school, including
the payments for school pence, has amounted to
£3060 19s. 6d.'[2]   At the height of the crisis, the total

[1] *Reports of Factory Inspectors : Parl. Pap.* 1864, XXII, p. 618.

[2] *Ibid.,* p. 683.   *Cf.* also : ' The extraordinary benevolence called into
existence at that period has never been exceeded in the annals of Christian
philanthropy.   America contributed largely to the general relief funds,

number of adults and children attending school must have been very great. Full statistics for Lancashire, where the effect of the stoppage of the mills was greatest are not given in Factory Inspectors' reports ; but in Redgrave's district, which included Yorkshire, the number in January 1863 was not less than 80,000. During that year, however, a considerable improvement in the situation took place, so that by the end of the year the number had fallen to 28,000, of whom 18,000 were children.[1]

and the liberality displayed by many noble and generous men of our own country was marvellous. During the whole period of the Cotton Famine, the following contributions were handed in to the Lancashire Committee : Central Relief Fund, £892,279 ; Mansion House Fund, £503,131 ; Cotton Districts, £254,380 ; General Subscriptions, £283,989 ; and General Contributions, £40,434 ; making the enormous total of £1,974,203.' *The Cotton Famine* (1872), p. 6.

[1] *Reports of Factory Inspectors . Parl. Pap.* 1864, XXII, p. 622. The following song was popular at the time among the operatives (*Reports of Factory Inspectors : Parl. Pap.* 1863, XVIII, p. 479). It described, wrote one of the factory inspectors, in the operatives' own language, what their masters are doing for them ; it expressed also their appreciation of the gifts they receive, their sense of the sufficiency of the relief, and the cheerfulness in waiting for better times :

OUR FACTORY SCHOOL

By Elijah Moss

You factory folks of Lancashire, a song we'll sing to you,
Of a school now formed at Higher Hurst, and every word is true
Our masters are determined to care well for their hands,
If they will only come to school, and there obey commands.

Chorus

Then old and young attend the school, your teachers there obey,
There's military exercise, and military pay.

Our mules and looms have now ceased work, and Yankees are the cause
But we will let them fight it out and stand by English laws ;
No recognizing shall take place, until the war is o'er ;
Our wants are now attended to, we cannot ask for more.

Potatoes, ham, and bacon are now to us being sold,
With comforts such as these, we have no fear of winter cold ;
Every one seems hearty glad, and says with joyous glee,
For men and masters now do meet in love and unity.

Amongst our scholars there are some whose age is past threescore,
Who have for learning, wages, which they never had before ;
The pencils, slates, and copy books are free for us to use,
And every morning on each desk is laid the daily news.

A system of good order rules supreme from morn till night ;
There's grammar and arithmetic, and nearly all can write ;
Reciting too, with moral songs, to suit the gay or brave
And often do we close our school with singing " Sailor's Grave."

Now old and young forget your cares, and join in singing praise,
The time is not far distant when we shall have better days ;
Then comforts soon to everyone, with joy we shall abound,
Contentment, peace, and plenty may we have on British ground.

CHAPTER IV

EXTENSION TO OTHER TRADES AND MANUFACTURES— PRINT WORKS, LACE FACTORIES, BLEACHING AND DYEING WORKS

IN 1841, a Commission was appointed for inquiring into the employment and condition of children in mines and manufactures. The Commissioners appointed were Thomas Tooke and Dr Thomas Southwood Smith, who had taken a principal part in the Factory Inquiry Commission of 1833, together with Leonard Horner and Robert S. Saunders, the two leading Factory Inspectors.[1] These four constituted the Central Board, sub-commissioners being appointed to carry out the investigation in different districts covering the whole of the United Kingdom. The object of the Commission, it was explained in the instructions issued by the Central Board to the sub-commissioners,[2] was to inquire into the employment and condition of all children of the poorer classes, not under the protection of the Factory Regulation Act, who were employed in any description of mining and manufacturing labour whatsoever, in which they worked together in numbers. By the term ' children ' was to be understood those who had not completed their thirteenth year. The main duty of the sub-commissioners was to collect the most full and complete

[1] *Children's Employment Commission : Second Report, Parl. Pap.* 1843, XIII, p. 309.
[2] *Ibid.*, p. 534.

evidence which it was practicable to obtain, as to the number and nature of those employments, the distinguishing peculiarities of each, and the nature and extent of the evils which might result to the children, whether from the tenderness of their age, the peculiarities of sex, the severity or duration of their labour, the insufficiency of their food and clothing, the inadequate time allowed for their meals, or the absence of any opportunity during the twenty-four hours for healthful recreation, and for religious, moral and intellectual culture.

' You will inquire ', the instructions went on to state, ' in what numbers, at what ages, and for how many hours per week, the children attend day schools ; and endeavour to obtain from the teachers an account of the methods of instruction pursued, the books used, and whether the girls are instructed in needle and other household work in these schools. You will learn whether any and what provisions are made in them for training the children in moral habits, for affording them religious knowledge. . . .

' You will ascertain the expense of school attendance ; by whom the money is paid ; and the degree in which the attendance of the child is interrupted by ignorance, poverty, negligence or selfishness on the part of the parents ; and, by a personal examination of the children in the several establishments which you visit, you will learn the extent to which they appear to have profited by their attendance at school.

' You will collect information as to the station, salaries, knowledge, and qualifications of the teachers, and especially whether they have themselves received any training for their office ; if so where, and with what methods of instruction they are acquainted.

' You will in every instance inquire whether any school is connected with the works you visit ; what interest is taken in the education of the children by the employers or parents, or their indifference to it ; and the capacity or inaptitude of the children for receiving instruction after their hours of labour.'

PRINT WORKS

The investigation of the conditions in the calico print works of Lancashire was assigned to Mr J. L. Kennedy The children were found to be engaged chiefly in the processes of ' block-printing ' and ' teering '. The operations were described as follows : ' The children spread the cotton evenly on a woollen sieve with a small hand-brush ; this done, the block-printer places his block in the sieve, and serves it with colour ; he then applies it to the cloth, giving it a slight tap with the mall or mallet which he holds in his left hand. During the time which is occupied in applying the block to the cloth, the teerer draws his brush over the sieve and lays on the colour evenly as before, to be ready for the next serving of the block. There is one teerer to each block-printer. . . . His work is easy and does not require much muscular exertion, and the monotony of the work is considerably relieved by his having to bring the colour from the colour shop, and from its being part of his duty to clean the blocks and sieves.' ' The objections to the employment of very young children in print grounds,' wrote Kennedy, ' do not appear to me to apply to the nature of their employment, but rather to the long and very irregular hours, both in the night and day, during which they are obliged to work, which at a very tender age deprives them of the chance of relaxation at that period of life when the frame most requires it ; and in addition to this, takes away the opportunity of cultivating and developing their intellectual powers.'[1] Children were also found to be employed in other departments of the works ; in the dye house, ' the most disagreeable department by far . . . the floor is always wet, and steam from the different processes escapes in great quantities ' ; and in singeing, in which the cloth was drawn over a red-hot cylinder to burn off the nap on the surface—' the singeing room is filled with small burnt particles, which irritate the nostrils and eyes exceedingly.'   The usual hours of work were from six in the morning to six and sometimes eight o'clock in the evening ; but in all the departments the hours were found to be irregular.

Out of 565 children taken at random, the age at which they first began work was found to be as shown in the following table :—

5 years and under	Between 5 & 6	Between 6 & 7	Between 7 & 8	Between 8 & 9	Between 9 & 10	Between 10 &11	Between 11 &12	Between 12 &13	Total
1	3	68	133	156	127	49	26	2	565

Thus nearly two-thirds began before they were nine years old.

In the print works in the parts of Lancashire covered by Kennedy, 3616 boys and 2030 girls under thirteen years of age were employed.   Many of those who claimed to be

[1] *Children's Employment Commission.   Appendix to Second Report :*
Parl. Pap. 1843, XIV, pp. B7 *et seq.*

able to read were found wanting when put to a test. Only 365 of the boys and 56 of the girls could write their names. As illustrating the general state of education in the towns affected, Kennedy referred to information which had recently been ascertained concerning Manchester. About one-third of the estimated number of children between the ages of five and fifteen years in Manchester —50,000—were receiving no instruction at all, about one half were receiving instruction in Sunday schools only, and two-thirds of the whole were attending Sunday schools, or day schools, or both. Of the teachers only 65 out of 598 had been educated with the express view of becoming teachers. ' This,' remarked Kennedy, ' is a great defect in our educational system (if we can be said to have one). It seems to be a profession which none betake themselves to except as a last resource. . . . The care and education of the young not unfrequently devolve upon those whose tempers are soured by misfortune, and who are consequently least of all fitted for that important task. Nothing seems to be more desirable than a school for the education of teachers. . . . School teaching is a great art, if not a gift, and upon the ability of the teachers the progress of the scholars mainly depends.'

In giving his general conclusions, Kennedy referred to the need for new and adequate provisions for an efficient education being made, and measures being taken to enforce the attendance of the children at school. To restrict the hours of employment without some such preliminary provision, he considered, would be merely to turn the children into the streets, to engender habits of idleness, or to send them to their homes where there would be no provision for their training or education and where too they would have no advantage in respect of health over the factories. But the difference between a good and a bad population depended on education being given, and on this account, he concluded, it was absolutely requisite that the hours of work of the children should be shortened.

On 18th February, 1845, Lord Ashley endeavoured in the House of Commons to bring in a Bill to deal with the employment of these children. The Commissioners had stated in their general report, he said, that the evidence collected in the Lancashire district had tended to show that the children employed in print works were excluded from the opportunities of education ; that the ease of obtaining early employment in this occupation emptied the day schools ; and that the parents without hesitation sacrificed the future welfare of their children through life for the immediate advantage or gratification obtained by the additional pittance derived from the child's earning. He intended to propose the total abolition of night work for all females of whatsoever ages, and all of both sexes under thirteen. He would propose that in October 1846 none under thirteen years of age should be allowed to work more than eight hours a day for six days in the week, or more than thirteen hours a day for three alternate days in the week. He would propose also, in conformity with the provisions of the Factory Act, that two hours a day of schooling should be required with respect to those children who worked for eight hours a day for six days a week ; and three hours of schooling, on alternate days, with respect to those children who worked twelve hours a day for three days a week.[1] Sir James Graham, the Home Secretary, met

[1] See *Hansard* 1845, LXXVII, pp. 638-668 for debate.

this in cold fashion. Though not approving the introduc
tion of a Bill, he reserved ' the most perfect latitude and
discretion as to the mode in which the proposition shall
be dealt with.' He saw the impossibility, if they now
advanced on this line, of stopping there. Lord Ashley
had indeed made clear that he did not mean to stop there.
This Sir James Graham could not view without a serious
apprehension that a fatal effect would be produced on the
trade and manufactures of the country.

The Bill[1] was read a first time on 12th March, 1845, and
came up for a second reading on 2nd April.[2] The Factory
Inspectors, it was proposed, should have the same powers
and duties in respect to print works as they already
exercised in respect to the factories covered by the Factory
Acts. Children under eight years should not be employed
at all in the print works. Clauses giving effect to the
proposals for the restriction of hours, and for the attendance
of the children at school, as Lord Ashley had described,
were included. The attendance at school should be
certified by the master of the school attended, and all the
provisions and regulations then in force under the Factory
Acts respecting the retention by the factory owners of
these certificates, the deduction of a sum not exceeding 2d.
per week from the wages of the child for payment to the
schoolmaster, the allowing or annulling of the certificates
by the Inspectors, should in all respects be applicable to the
school attendance of the children employed in print works.
Provision was made for penalties on the employers for

---

[1] *Bill to Regulate the Labour of Children in Calico Print Works : Parl.
Pap.* 1845, I, pp. 227-235.

[2] See *Hansard* 1845, LXXVIII, pp. 1369-1389 for debate.

employing children under thirteen years without the
certificates, and on parents for allowing their children to
neglect attending school. The Bill included in the term
' Print works ' the processes of ' printing, dyeing, bleaching
or calendering any cotton, linen or woollen fabric '.

To the provision that the Bill should extend to dyeing,
bleaching and calendering, Sir James Graham offered
strong resistance. As regards education, he referred to
the peculiar nature of the industry in regard to the
fluctuations in demands and consequently in employment.
At certain times when the demand was extraordinary,
elasticity in the regulations as to hours of employment
would be necessary. Graham put the total of the periods
of intense demand at eight months in the year. ' In
deciding on the question of the leave to be allowed for the
education of the children employed in these works, I would
prefer looking to the analogy between their conditions and
that of the children of agricultural labourers, rather than
to that of factory labour regulated by machinery. In the
north of England and in Scotland, where it is well known
the children of agricultural labourers are, practically
speaking, well educated,[1] there are certain periods of the
year when, in consequence of the greater demand for
labour, there is a suspension of education. . . . Now . . .
having assumed that during eight months out of the twelve
the work should continue day by day in these establishments while the work is comparatively light during the
other four months, I would propose that the days for
education should be regulated accordingly. We could
secure a provision under this enactment, that during 100
days throughout the year, being about one-third of the

[1] *Cf. infra*, pp. 173, 177.

I

whole working year, all children employed in these works from eight to thirteen years of age should attend a school daily, as in the case of the factory children, say for three or four hours a day ; and I would also recommend, in order that there may be no evasion of the intention of the legislature, that this period should be divided into fifty days in each half-year.'

This offer on the part of the Government, Lord Ashley, remarking that as struggle on his part would be nearly hopeless, agreed to accept ; and with these limitations, which made the Bill far less comprehensive and effectual than Lord Ashley's original draft, the Measure passed through both Houses, and received the Royal Assent on 30th June, 1845.

It is of interest to note that in the discussion on the Bill in the House of Lords, Lord Brougham said that he could not refrain from entering his protest against insisting, year after year, on thus legislating, in the wrong direction. Professing great concern for the working classes, they were doing all they could by their legislation to injure and oppress them, and were treating them with what he held to be mere cruelty, under the false garb and guise of humanity.[1]

[1] Brougham had introduced a Bill in 1820 for the levying of a compulsory rate for educational purposes. Later, however, he modified his views. ' I think that [general education, established by law],' he told the Select Committee on the State of Education in 1834, ' is wholly inapplicable to the present condition of the country . . . If the State were to interfere, and obliged every parish to support a school or schools sufficient for educating all children, two consequences would inevitably follow : the greater part of the funds now raised voluntarily for this purpose would be withdrawn ; and the state or the ratepayers in each parish would have to provide schools for 2,000,000 children, because the interference would be quite useless, unless it supplied the whole defect . . . That the funds now raised by subscription, and which amount to near a million a year,

The Printworks Act[1] generally was to take effect from 1st January, 1846, and the education clauses from 1st July, 1846. The clauses relating to hours of employment, the requiring of certificates of age—' surgical certificates '—, the duties and powers of the Inspectors, the keeping of registers of children employed, the issue of a summons for offences against the Act, the penalties, and the like, followed very much those of the Factory Act of the preceding year. The main school clauses were as follows :

' 23. After the first day of July, 1846, the parent or person having any direct benefit from the wages of any child employed or intended to be employed in a print work shall cause such child to attend some school for at least thirty days, together or separately, exclusive of Sundays, during the half-year between the first day of January and the thirtieth day of June, both days inclusive, and in like manner for thirty days during the half-year between the first day of July and the thirty-first day of December, both days inclusive, in each year, during any part of which it shall be employed in a printwork, such attendance being after the hour of eight o'clock in the morning and before the hour of six o'clock in the evening, and such attendance shall not be less than one hundred and fifty hours during each half

will entirely fail, I take to be the inevitable consequence of establishing a school rate. All will think they will do enough by paying that, and be ready to relieve themselves of both trouble and expense, when the Government shall have taken the whole on itself. To which I must add, that my belief is, that a surer way to make education unpopular, and thus arrest its progress, could not be devised, than making it the cause either of a general tax, or of an increase in the parish rate.' For an account of Brougham's views on, and work for education, see *Lord Brougham and the Whig Party*, Aspinall A. (1927), pp. 231-9.

[1] 8 and 9 Vict., c. 29.

year ; but no attendance above five hours on any one day shall be reckoned as part of the said one hundred and fifty hours.

‘ 24. That so soon as a child shall be employed in a printwork the parent or person having direct benefit from the wages of such child shall notify to the occupiers of the printwork the school which such child is to attend during the time it is employed in such printwork, and the occupiers of the printwork shall enter in the register of children hereinafter required to be kept the name of the schoolmaster and the situation of the school so notified to him ; and the parent or person having direct benefit from the wages of such child shall provide a School Certificate book, according to the form and directions given in the schedule annexed to this Act, and shall deliver the same to the master of the school where such child is to attend, and the said master shall enter therein, week by week, the attendance or absence of such child during that week, and shall produce such Certificate Book, while in his custody, to the Inspector or Sub-Inspector of the District, when required ; and the master of any school which shall be attended by children employed in a printwork shall keep a register of their names and attendance, and if the Inspector of the District shall disapprove of the form of register adopted by the schoolmaster, it shall be kept in such other form as the Inspector shall direct.

‘ 25. After the first day of July, 1846, the occupiers of every printwork shall, before employing any child therein, obtain from a schoolmaster a certificate, according to the form and directions given in the schedule to this Act annexed, that such child had attended school for at least fifty days, as required by this Act, during the half-year ending on the thirtieth day of June or the thirty-first day of December next before the beginning of such employment and the like certificate at the beginning of each following period of six months during which the employment of such child shall be continued in that printwork ; and such occupier shall keep every such certificate so long as such child shall continue in his employment for twelve months after the date thereof, and shall produce the same to any Inspector or Sub-Inspector, when required, during such period.'

The Inspectors were required to keep full minutes of all such visits and proceedings and to report the same and the state and condition of the printworks and of the children employed therein to the Secretary of State twice a year. As in the case of the Factory Acts, the penalties paid by offenders were to be applied by the Inspectors for the ' establishment or support of day schools for the education of children employed in printworks.'

The insertion in clause 25 of the Act of the word ' fifty ' as the number of days on which the children must have attended school was made in error. ' Thirty ' had been intended, and it was necessary to pass an amending Act[1] the following year—' an Act to amend two clerical errors in an Act of the last Session, for regulating the labour of children, young persons, and women in printworks '—in order to regularise the procedure.

The requirement as to a child's having attended school for at least thirty days during the half-year ending on 30th June or on 31st December before commencing employment was soon found to present great difficulty, especially

[1] 9 Vict., c. 18.

in obtaining the requisite proof of previous school attendance. Saunders reported that he felt the latter to be very oppressive and that consequently he had countenanced a departure from the letter of the law to the extent of permitting employment where the required number of days at school had been put in, though not necessarily during the half-year mentioned in the Act.[1] The number of children employed in printworks soon, in fact, fell very considerably, their places being taken doubtless by young persons over thirteen years of age. The reduction was assisted by the substitution during the next few years of machine printing for block printing. Nor does the Act appear to have done very much for those children who remained in employment in the printworks. Their hours of work were not restricted, except that they could not be employed before 6 a.m. or after 10 p.m. Their attendance at school—during thirty days in each half-yearly period— could be completed as irregularly as the school would tolerate, and the period of attendance was sometimes for one hour only. Faced with these facts, the Inspectors, in a joint report at the end of 1846, pressed on the Government the desirability of remedying these shortcomings in the Act.[2]

In the following year, therefore, a further Act was passed.[3] The clauses 23, 24 and 25 of the Act of 1845 were repealed and provision was made for the minimum daily period of attendance at school to be two hours and a half and for the six months of school attendance required before a child could begin employment in a printworks to

[1] *Reports of Factory Inspectors : Parl. Pap.* 1847, XV, p. 787.
[2] *Reports of Factory Inspectors : Parl. Pap.* 1847, XV, p. 827.
[3] 10 and 11 Vict., c. 70.

reckon from the date of entering into employment instead
of being in respect of the preceding half-year ending 30th
June or 31st December. The operative clause was as
follows :—

' 3. After the first day of August [1847] the occupier
of every printwork shall, before employing any child
therein, obtain from a schoolmaster a certificate, according to one of the forms and according to the directions
given in the schedule to this Act annexed, that such
child had attended school for at least thirty days and
not less than one hundred and fifty hours during the
half-year immediately preceding the first day of the
employment of such child or if it shall have left the said
printworks and shall be again employed therein, the
said school attendance shall have been during the
half-year immediately preceding the first day of such
re-employment, and such school attendance shall be
after the hour of eight o'clock in the morning, and before
the hour of six o'clock in the evening, but no attendance
of less than two and a half hours on any one day shall be
reckoned as any part of the said one hundred and fifty
hours, nor shall any attendance on any one day for more
than five hours ; and a like certificate shall be obtained
at the beginning of each period of six calendar months
during whioh the employment of such child shall keep
every such certificate so long as such child shall continue
in his employment for twelve calendar months after the
date thereof, and shall produce the same to any Inspector
or Sub-Inspector when required during such period.'

It was in Lancashire that the greatest number of printworks were found. In Saunders's district, on the other
hand, there were only 46 printworks all told, and at only

six of these were children employed in 1849. The largest of these works was one at West Ham, employing 82 children. The Act was found to be strictly complied with, the registers to be kept in excellent order, and a complete system to be practised for checking any improper employment. Yet an examination of the records showed that the attendance at school of the children was very desultory. They attended for 150 hours during a period of six consecutive weeks, and were then employed in the factory for the remainder of the half-year without any school attendance at all. On returning to school after twenty weeks' absence, it could hardly be expected that they would remember much of what had been learned previously.[1] The Reverend W. J. Kennedy, one of H.M. Inspectors of Schools in Lancashire, writing to Horner about this period, remarked on the irregularity of the attendance of the printworks children, adding, ' The result unmistakably is that they are inferior in attainments to any other class of children in the schools I inspect.'[2]

The number of children employed in this industry, however, continued to fall. In 1855 Horner reported that in his district there were 721 children fewer than there had been five years before.[3]

Another of the Inspectors, T. J. Howell, was scathing in his remarks on the certificate of school attendance in the case of the printworks children. ' Estimated at its bare value [it] is not worth the paper on which it is written ; perhaps it is not worth so much, as it tends to spread the

[1] *Reports of Factory Inspectors : Parl. Pap.* 1850, XXIII, p. 232.
[2] *Reports of Factory Inspectors : Parl. Pap.* 1852-3, XL, pp. 546, 547.
[3] *Reports of Factory Inspectors : Parl. Pap.* 1856, XVIII, p. 233.

fallacy that a certificate of attendance at school for 150 hours in the course of a half-year, at the broken intervals which a child between eight and thirteen can snatch, who is allowed to work 16 hours out of the 24 without stopping, is evidence of some progress in the attainment of useful knowledge.'[1]

There were, however, one or two exceptions, where the proprietors of printworks had themselves established schools on the premises, or had taken active steps to promote the education of the children. Shortly after the Act of 1845 had been passed, Messrs. Hargreaves of Accrington, had issued a notice in the neighbourhood, which contained the following paragraphs :—

'It is a main object of this law that the teerers and other children employed in printworks should get some education on the week days, in addition to that they may receive in Sunday schools.

'It has been so contrived that the children may go to school during slack times, so as to interfere as little as possible with their work in brisk times.

'With a view to the better education of the children, it has been determined by Messrs. Hargreaves to give a preference of employment in slack times to those children who have made the most time at school beyond the 30 days required by the Act.'

Messrs. Margerisons and Co. also issued a handbill in which it was notified that :—

'Arrangements have been made, with the trustees of the Habersham-Eaves Parochial School at Sandy Gate and the National School belonging to the new

---

[1] *Reports of Factory Inspectors : Parl. Pap.* 1856, XVIII, p. 249.

district of St James', Burnley, whereby we have agreed
to pay the school for all children in our employ, who in
addition to the 30 days required by the Act, will have
the benefit of gratuitous instruction during the time
when they may not be employed at the works ; of
which privilege it is our particular request that the
parents will see that the children avail themselves.
Free tickets to the above schools will be given to such
children as are in our employ on application to the
counting house.'[1]

The Inspectors, reporting jointly in 1855, noted that
there had been some instances of the owners of printworks
having provided good schools and that in such cases, and
when the attendance of the children was carefully looked
after and they were not stinted to the legal minimum of
attendance, the schooling might do good.   But in practice,
as regarded the great majority of these children, the
attendance at school was merely a farce.   They gave it
as their view that there was nothing in the nature of the
employment of the children to prevent their labour being
restricted, as in the factories, to half a day, with a regular
attendance at school of three hours a day for five days a
week ; and added that an amendment of this part of the
Printworks Act was much needed.[2]   In 1857, Redgrave
reported that in one establishment ' the extreme periods
allowed by the law were the only limits of school attendance, viz., from 8 a.m. to 6 p.m. ; between those hours it
appeared from an examination of the certificate books that
the school was open, with the exception of an interval in
the middle of the day.   Sometimes a child would attend

---

[1] *Reports of Factory Inspectors : Parl. Pap.* 1847, XV, p. 787.
[2] *Reports of Factory Inspectors : Parl. Pap.* 1856, XVIII, p. 326.

school for the number of hours required by the law at one period of the day, sometimes at another period, but never regularly ; for instance, the attendance on one day might be from 8 a.m. to 11 a.m., on another day from 1 p.m. to 4 p.m., and the child might not appear at school again for several days when it would attend perhaps from 3 p.m. to 6 p.m. ; then it might attend for three or four days consecutively or for a week, then it would not appear in school for three weeks or a month, after that, upon some odd days at some odd hours when the operative who employed it chose to spare it ; and thus the child was, as it were, buffetted from school to work, from work to school, until the tale of 150 hours was told '.[1]

Even with the Factories Act Extension Act of 1864,[2] however, the law relating to printworks remained unaltered, although, as Baker remarked in his report of that year, ' it has been stated again and again in the Factory Inspectors' reports that the educational clauses of the Printworks Act of 1845 were comparatively worthless and that the labour of even very young children of eight years and upwards might be continued as late as ten o'clock at night '.[3] Notwithstanding the Factory Inspectors' reports however, it was not until 1870 that the provisions of the Factory Acts were applied to printworks.[4]

LACE FACTORIES

In connection with the Children's Employment Commission, the investigation of the employment of children in the manufacture of lace was chiefly undertaken by one

---

[1] *Reports of Factory Inspectors : Parl. Pap.* 1857, III, p. 599.
[2] *Cf. infra*, p. 194.
[3] *Reports of Factory Inspectors : Parl. Pap.* 1864, XXII, p. 762,
[4] *Cf. infra*, p. 203.

of the sub-commissioners, R. D. Grainger, who was assigned for this purpose to the Nottingham, Derby and Leicester districts. Though not able to state precisely the aggregate number of children employed,[1] Grainger reported that he believed that almost all the children of the labouring classes in Nottingham were engaged at a very early age in one or other of the several branches of the lace-manufacture and hosiery trade, ' as soon as they can tie a knot or use a needle ' ;[2] and it was much the same in the Leicester and Derby districts. Many boys were employed to assist men in working hand machines, or, where the machine was propelled by a wheel, to take the entire charge of it. Turning the wheel was very laborious work, especially when, as was frequently the case, it continued at all hours of the night (' no distinction in this respect being made in favour of the children '). In the case of both the hand-machines and the power-machines it was indispensable that at the same time the eyes should follow the work incessantly, in order to detect, and immediately to remedy, any errors which might occur ; the effect of this being in course of time severely to affect the eyesight of those engaged. Boys were often employed in the less strenuous work of minding the power-machines, though to a less extent than in the case of hand-machines. The process of ' threading ' occupied a very large number of children, mostly boys ; ' winding ', a smaller number, mostly girls. The result of 25 cases taken indiscriminately

---

[1] *Report of Census of* 1841 (*Occupation Abstract*)—5616 females and 1072 males under the age of 20 employed in lace manufacture in England. *Parl. Pap.* 1844, XXVII, p. 37.

[2] *Children's Employment Commission : Appendix to Second Report : Parl. Pap.* 1843, XIV, F 1 *et seq.*

from amongst the evidence collected by Grainger showed
that the average age at which children began to ' thread '
was about eight and a half years of age.   By the age of
fifteen the girls became ' winders ' or went to other occupations, and the boys then or earlier usually went to the
machines.   It was quite common for boys and girls to
begin as young as six and seven years, and many at five.
In one case a child was placed at work by the parent before
it was two—a fact, Grainger remarked, he would have
hesitated to report unless he had obtained a personal
knowledge of it.   With very few exceptions, the children
employed as ' threaders ' were liable to be called upon
during the whole time the machines were at work, whether
this was during 16, 20 or 22 out of the 24 hours.
' Threading ' consisted of passing the end of the thread
through an aperture, into the bobbin.   In the most
common kind of bobbin, the aperture was sufficiently large
to allow the thread to be drawn through it by means of a
small hook ; but in one type the opening or eye was so
small that it had to be threaded like a needle.   Some idea
of the nature of the occupation may be formed from the
facts that the average number of bobbins to be threaded
for one machine was about 1800, and the number of
threaders engaged, taking about two to two and a half
hours, was usually two or three.   And although subject
to harassing employment, and although it often happened
that the children employed in ' threading ' were kept
waiting in the factories and shops until actually required,
no provision was anywhere made for them to lie down or
sleep during the sometimes lengthy intervals in the nights ;
they were obliged to sleep on the floor, ' if there is room ',

or under the table, or on the old jackets belonging to the men. ' It is in such cases ', added Grainger, ' no exaggeration to affirm that these boys are in a Christian country treated as if they were mere brute animals '. In some of the better regulated factories there were rules according to which no machine was to be threaded after a certain hour at night, and more rarely not before a certain hour in the morning But even with these restrictions, the children were kept till 10 or 11 p.m., and were required at 4 or 5 a.m.

Every witness under eighteen examined by Grainger was questioned regarding his education. Many could neither read nor write ; the majority were able to read, and a limited number to write. But of those who could read, only a very small proportion did so otherwise than in a most mechanical and imperfect way. ' In by far the greatest number of instances they did not comprehend either the meaning of many of the words or the sense of the entire passage '. On visiting many of the schools, added Grainger, ' nothing could be more painful than to hear the children read in rotation passages usually taken from the scriptures. In the majority of instances this exercise consisted of nothing but the monotonous and usually discordant utterance of articulate sounds '. A large proportion of the children attended, or had attended, Sunday schools only, and in the great majority of these, reading in the Scriptures or religious books was the only instruction given. Inevitably such children had no knowledge of writing or ' accounts '. Indeed very few of the children examined by Grainger ' could write in a useful manner ', whilst ' as regards any general information even

of the most limited kind, such as the situation of Scotland,
the names of the four quarters of the globe, etc., I do not
think that more than a dozen . . . had any knowledge at
all upon the subject. Of the history of their own country
little or nothing was known '. Where children had
attended day schools, the period had been very brief. All
the teachers who were questioned complained that the
children were constantly being withdrawn to go to work
at a very early age. One mistress stated that if trade
became brisk, ' in a fortnight half the school would leave '.
The evidence of the master of the Boys' National School
in Nottingham was as follows :—

' The boys who attend are from 6 to 10 years of age :
there are very few above that age. The number in
attendance greatly fluctuates, which witness attributes
to this being a manufacturing town. During the last
12 months about 340 boys have on the whole been in the
school . . . The average number of boys in attendance
is 220. . . . They are withdrawn from the school on
the average at nine, to go to work. A larger number,
however, leave younger, to go as ' seamers and runners '.
Some have left for this purpose as young as seven. If
trade is good the number in attendance is considerably
diminished. . . . Is of opinion the boys cannot receive
a sound education so long as they are withdrawn at so
early an age into the factory. The majority who leave
can read the New Testament, not the Old ; and also
write on slates.'

Nearly twenty years, however, were to elapse before
legislative action to remedy the deplorable state of affairs
in the lace industry disclosed by the Children's Employment

Commission, was to be taken. In 1846 an unsuccessful attempt was made to do so, a Bill being introduced in the House of Commons by Thomas Duncombe and John Fielden.[1] The main proposals of this Bill were :—the prohibition of the employment of children under eight years of age in connection with the making of lace on bobbin-net and warp-lace machines ' in any factory, shop or other premises or dwelling house ' ; such machines not to be worked except between the hours of 6 a.m. and 10 p.m. and except between these hours no person to work on them, on penalty, on the proprietor being convicted before the magistrates, of a sum not exceeding £50 nor less than £30. No provisions concerning the education of the children were included. In moving the second reading of his Bill,[2] Duncombe gave the number of children affected as 2,450. Sir James Graham, the Home Secretary, again showed his opposition to the reform of factory employment. In a long and, in parts, rather disingenuous speech,[3] he attempted to justify resistance to the Bill by showing that the condition of the working classes concerned would be worsened, and not improved. Referring to the evidence taken by the Children's Employment Commission, he said, ' It will be found that the principal causes which are there enumerated, of the evil effects of over-work and long hours upon children, are not in the case of factories wrought by power, but in the private workshops and even in the private dwelling-houses of the hand-loom weavers, who are the competitors of the power-loom weavers. . . . Now

---

[1] *Bill to Regulate the Hours of Night Labour in all Factories where Bobbin-Net and Warp Lace Machinery is Employed : Parl. Pap.* 1846, II, p. 177.
[2] *Hansard* 1846, LXXXVI, pp. 916, 917.
[3] *Ibid.*, pp. 918-926.

the House, I think, will pause before they introduce a principle so new . . . that actually your report of inspection or regulations shall extend to the dwelling-houses of the labourers themselves.' Yet so far as Grainger's report was concerned, there was no lack of evidence of the evil conditions in the lace factories, and little or no reference in it to hand-loom working in private houses. Graham's views as to hours of work and as to the physical nature of the work, too, were far from according with those of the sub-commissioner. ' I am not informed that in any case the machinery runs continuously from the Monday morning till the Saturday night : on the contrary, I believe that the utmost length of time in twenty-four hours, for which machinery runs, is twenty hours, and that whenever the machinery runs for twenty hours out of the twenty-four, the labour is by spells, by reliefs, no person working above eight hours continuously ; and with reference to children, the labour is remarkably light, and not continuous.' Using an argument he had brought forward on earlier occasions, he referred to the prospect that interference with private labour might extend. ' What do you say to the pin maker, the nail maker, the fustian cutter ? You cannot stop short : if you begin to regulate the intensity of competition, there will be no species of labour with which you will not interfere by legislation. And when you do that, you will affect the earnings of labour ; and you cannot, in justice to the workmen, stop short of the establishment of a minimum wage. That will be the inevitable consequence ; and what then ? Why, capital will " make to itself wings, and fly away ". . . . The commencement of this career will be the downfall of our manufacturing prosperity : and I hold that we have

K

arrived at a stage in our social condition, when the downfall of our manufacturing prosperity will be the loss of our position among the nations of the earth.' Inaccurate as were some of his statements and fallacious as were some of his arguments Graham's speech produced the desired effect. The mistake had been made in the Bill of providing for the regulation of the employment of adults as well as of children, and though in this connection Duncombe expressed his willingness to have the Bill amended in Committee, the House would have none of it, the rejection of the Bill being carried by 151 votes to 66.

So the employment of children in the lace industry remained unregulated for another sixteen years.[1] Towards the end of 1860, the then Home Secretary, Sir George Cornewall Lewis, instructed Hugh Seymour Tremenheere

---

[1] *Cf.* a pamphlet *The Lace Trade and the Factory Act* (1860) : ' That some lace children do occasionally attend Sunday school is true ; but go into any Sunday school in Nottingham, and you cannot fail to distinguish the children who work at a lace factory from those who are employed under the protection of the Factory Act. The lace children are the most backward in the school. There they sit, boys and girls of ten, eleven, and thirteen years of age, languishing in " pale decay ", far back upon the lowest forms, and vainly trying to fix their attention on the books before them . . . Energies they have none . . . And yet these children, and there are thousands in their position, have natural gifts and dormant faculties which instruction might tend to develop and call forth, if we could only obtain for them the protection of a law of the land '. Quoted in *Suggestions on Popular Education*, Senior, N. W. (1861), p. 222. Senior was born in 1790. Called to the Bar in 1819. Became interested in political economy, and in 1825 was chosen as the first holder of the Professorship of Political Economy at Oxford. Was a member of the Poor Law Commission in 1833, and served later on a Factory Commission, the Handloom Commission of 1841, the Irish Poor Law Commission of 1844, and the Education Commission of 1851. ' Merits a fuller biography than the authoritative but brief note in the *Dictionary of National Biography* and that in Boase's *Modern English Biography*.' (*English Poor Law History* : Part II (1929), Webb, S. and B., p. 48).

to make the enquiry whether it would be expedient to subject the lace trade to regulations similar to those of the Factory Acts. Tremenheere after an extensive inquiry in the Nottingham district reported to the Home Secretary in March 1861.[1] During the interval since the Children's Employment Commission had investigated the matter nearly twenty years before, the hand-machines worked in private houses had been almost completely displaced by steam power-machines collected into factories. The evidence showed that the women, young persons, and children were still employed according to the system described in Grainger's report of 1842 and that, although in some factories, and at times of depressed trade, the hours of attendance at or within call of the factory were reduced, at others the long hours of night work continued. The number of children under thirteen years of age employed, however, had fallen considerably, and was estimated to be about 600.[2] Some of the employers, strongly averse from the prospect of the industry being subjected to the provisions of the Factory Acts, urged that a far better way of dealing with the position would be to pass a general Education Act, applicable to all industrial employments.[3]

[1] *Report upon the Expediency of Subjecting the Lace Manufacture to the Regulations of the Factory Acts : Parl. Pap.* 1861, XXII.

[2] *Ibid.*, p. 573.

In Nottingham and district (including Derbyshire)	Boys	274
	Girls	120
		——394
In West of England	Boys	101
	Girls	106
		——207
	Total	601

[3] *Ibid.*, p. 538. Evidence of Mr Heymann, ' Chairman of the Committee of masters appointed with reference to the proposed legislation for lace factories'.

Many of the employers had said that rather than be at the trouble of keeping books and registers required by the Factory Acts for ' half-timers ', they would discharge all children under thirteen.   To this, however, Tremenheere answered that it was to the interest of the employer to train children from their first going to work to the processes of threading and winding, in order to give them the manual skill required, and that it was a disadvantage to the employers to have to bring children to that work from other forms of employment.   There was also another process, that of ' jacking off '—winding remnants of silk or cotton thread from the bobbins that had not been quite emptied when taken out of the machine—the earnings from which were so small that none but quite young children would undertake it.   This, then, was an additional reason why it was unlikely that the threat to discharge the children would be carried out.

Tremenheere accordingly recommended that from and after 1st August, 1862, the Factory Acts, with two minor modifications, should be applied to the lace industry.

This time it was not long before Parliament took action. A Bill[1] embodying Tremenheere's recommendation, with an important modification as regards age, was introduced on 31st May, 1861,[2] and given a second reading a week later.[3]   The modification mentioned would have had the effect of substituting the age of eleven years for that of thirteen prescribed in the Factories Acts, as the upper age of a child as defined by the Act ; and after reaching the

[1] *Bill to place the Employment of Women, Young Persons, and Children in Lace Factories under the Regulations of the Factories Acts : Parl. Pap.* 1861, III, p. 37.

[2] *Hansard* 1861, CLXIII, p. 373.

[3] *Ibid.*, p. 758.

age of eleven, they would have become ' young persons ',
working longer hours and not being subject to the provisions for compulsory education. An amendment was
accordingly proposed in committee by Lord Henry Lennox
to make the upper age for children thirteen years.[1] The
member for Nottingham (Mr Paget) endeavoured with
some show of ingenuity to argue that this was inconsistent
with a desire to promote the cause of education. Parents,
he said, could not be expected to give up the advantage of
their children's labour long after the time when the latter
were physically able to earn wages ; and the effect of the
Factory Acts in many instances had been that parents had
neglected the education of their children in their earlier
years, depending on the education which they would
receive later under the Factory Acts. If, however, a
parent received full wages from a child between the age
of eleven and thirteen he could afford to allow the younger
children to have an education up to the age of eleven.
Although Sir George Lewis informed the House that eleven
years had been prescribed in the Bill in accordance with
modified views to which Tremenheere had come since
making his report, and although Mr W. E. Forster
endeavoured to secure a compromise by suggesting that
the age might be twelve years (' they might begin at
twelve, and, perhaps, they would get to thirteen in a year
or two '), the amendment to make the age thirteen was
carried by a majority of four votes.[2] The Bill then had
a comparatively easy passage through both Houses, and
received the Royal Assent on 6th August, 1861. The
provisions of the Act[3] were to come into effect on 1st
August, 1862.

[1] *Hansard* 1861, CLXIV, p. 1441.   [2] *Ibid.*, p. 1446.   [3] 24/25 Vict., c. 117.

BLEACHING AND DYEING WORKS

According to the census report for 1841, there were employed in bleaching factories in England 774 males and 164 females under twenty years of age, and 2637 males and 90 females under that age in dyeing processes.[1] Kennedy, the sub-commissioner for Lancashire under the Children's Employment Commission, in the course of his investigations of 1841, found that a large number of young persons were employed in bleaching works in the neighbourhoods of Bolton, Bury, and Stockport,[2] and that in all these works a few children under thirteen were employed. The hours of work were very irregular, some weeks the workpeople being almost idle whilst in the following week they might have to work for 14 to 18 hours a day and occasionally all night. A few of the children were employed in the ' drying ' process, for which a high temperature which could not but be injurious to health was necessary ; but apart from this, the children seemed to be remarkably healthy compared with those employed in other trades. A considerable number of boys and girls were also employed in bleaching works in the Nottingham district, in connection with lace and hosiery goods.[3]

This was the position as ascertained in 1841 ; but a long time was to pass before Parliament was to legislate for the industry. Bleaching and dyeing works were not included in the scope of the Factories Act of 1844. Ten years later, in June and July of 1854, a Bill,[4] introduced by Lord

---

[1] *Census Report for* 1841 (*Occupation Abstract*) : *Parl. Pap.* 1844, XXVII, pp, 32, 34.

[2] Children's Employment Commission : *Appendix to the Second Report :* *Parl. Pap.* 1843, XIV, p. B43. [3] *Ibid.*, p. F16.

[4] *Bill to Regulate the Employment of Females, Young Persons, and Children in Bleaching, Finishing and Dyeing Works :* *Parl. Pap.* 1854, I, p. 217.

Shaftesbury,[1] passed the House of Lords, and was then brought at a later period of the session to the House of Commons.[2] ' Whereas it is expedient ', the preamble ran, ' to provide for the regulation of the hours of labour . . . in bleaching, finishing, and dyeing works . . . and whereas it is also expedient to give opportunity to the parents and guardians of children so employed to provide for their education.' It was proposed to prohibit the employment of children under ten years of age, and to limit the employment of women and of boys up to the age of eighteen to the hours between 6 a.m. and 6 p.m. The Factory Inspectors were to have power to enforce the carrying out of the regulations ; but no provision for the compulsory attendance at school of the children was made in the Bill. It did not, however, get beyond a first reading in the House of Commons. In introducing a similar bill in the House of Commons the following year, Mr I. Bute stated : ' In the Bill which came down from the House of Lords last year an objection was made against proceeding with it until an inquiry was instituted into the whole subject.'[3] Towards the end of the year, therefore, H. S. Tremenheere[4]

---

[1] *Hansard* 1855, CXXXIX, p. 1357.

[2] *Hansard* 1854, CXXXIV, pp. 478, 931 ; CXXXV, pp. 234, 316.

[3] *Hansard* 1855, CXXXIX, p. 1355.

[4] Hugh Seymour Tremenheere (1804-1893). Educated at Winchester and New College, Oxford, of which he was a Fellow from 1824 to 1856. Called to the Bar in 1834, and practised law for a few years. Appointed an Inspector of Schools in 1840, and an Assistant Poor Law Commissioner in 1842. As will be seen from the following pages, he was appointed the Commissioner under the Mines Act 1842, to inquire into the state of the population in the mining districts, rendering annual reports from 1843 to 1859. He was appointed in 1854 to undertake special inquiries into the conditions of employment in the bleaching trade, and, as is stated above, in 1860 to inquire into lace factories. From 1862 to 1867 he was one of the Commissioners appointed for inquiring into the conditions of employ-

was appointed a Commissioner to inquire how far it was desirable to extend the provisions of the Factory Act to bleaching works.[1] He found the hours of work to be long, though in some instances the employment was irregular From six and seven in the morning until eight, nine, and even ten o'clock at night was usual in works where employment was plentiful. The main facts, indeed, as regarded ' long hours ' were admitted by the masters ; but they replied that no harm was done in the great majority of cases, the occupation being a very healthy one. This view Tremenheere considered was subject to some important corrections. The various bleaching processes exposed the workpeople to much wet and damp, which at least in cold weather could not but be much felt by the boys. In the drying places, the temperatures had necessarily to be very high. It was a common expression, Tremenheere found, when any one was observed to be declining in health, to say, ' this work is too heavy for him (or her) ; he (or she) ought to be put to some lighter business '. Accordingly he stated, ' very confidently ', that ' in every one of the bleaching and finishing works I visited, and in which those ' long hours ' had been common, I observed very many boys, girls, young men and young women, both pale and sickly in their appearance, and stunted in their growth, and bearing evident marks in their general aspect of being injuriously affected by excess of labour.' There is a

ment of children and young persons in trades and manufactures, and from 1867 to 1870 for a similar inquiry in connection with agriculture. He retired from the public service in 1871. The *Dictionary of National Biography* records that Tremenheere was instrumental in bringing about fourteen Acts of Parliament, all having for their object the amelioration of the condition of the working classes.

[1] *Report of the Commissioner on Bleaching Works : Parl. Pap.* 1854-5, XVIII, p. 3.

modern touch in his view that if a bill were to be passed to limit the hours of work for women and boys the immediate effect would in all probability be to make the owners enlarge their works and improve their machinery : so keen was the competition, he wrote, that they would try to obtain the means of getting through the same amount of work in a given time as they could already do with the unlimited power to employ the women and boys for fifteen sixteen, eighteen or more hours per day. His conclusion therefore was that the hours established by the Factory Acts (viz., from 6 a.m. to 6 p.m., and a half holiday on Saturdays) might with propriety and safety be applied to the bleaching, finishing and dyeing works ; but if in any factories two hours were assigned for meals (one and a half hours was the time prescribed in the Factories Act) he thought the hour of employment might be extended from 6 p.m. to 6.30 p.m. As regarded the age of employment, his view was that a proposal that no child should be admitted to work under the age of eleven years would not be objected to. ' Previously to a child arriving at the age of eleven, there have been opportunities of school instruction which will in all probability, considering the growing disposition among the working classes towards education, and the greatly increased number and efficiency of schools, have been to a certain extent taken advantage of. To introduce a system of compulsory attendance for children of eleven years of age, which, according to the analogy of the Factory Act would only be of two years' duration, would probably be acknowledged to be inexpedient.'[1]

In the same month as Tremenheere's Report was issued —June 1855—a further bill, based substantially on the

[1] *Ibid.*, pp. 18, 19.

Report and prepared largely at the instigation of a committee of workmen employed in bleach-works, who were
anxious to see reforms brought about, was introduced
privately.[1] Sir George Grey, the Home Secretary, speaking
on 25th July, 1855, on the occasion of the second reading,
thought it was unfair on the part of the promoters to press
a measure of such importance at that late period of the
Parliamentary session. He hinted that further inquiry
might be needed (' reserving to himself full power and right
to consider . . . whether the inquiry had been so full and
complete as to render all further inquiry unnecessary '),
and made it clear that he would vote against the Bill
proceeding.   Although the House was fairly evenly
divided, the opponents of reform carried the day by the
narrow majority of five votes.[2] The promoters returned
to the charge in the following session, introducing in March,
1856, a new Bill[3] on similar lines to that of the preceding
year. As the Government were unable to give facilities
for the early discussion of the Bill, it was once more late
in the Parliamentary session before it came up for the
second reading. Again the opponents of the Measure
' deprecated proceeding with a Bill of this importance at
such a late period of the Session ',[4] and they found a
powerful supporter in the former Home Secretary, Sir
James Graham. For him the minimum of interference in

[1] *A Bill to Regulate the Employment of Females and Young Persons under
Eighteen in Bleaching, Finishing and Dyeing Works : Parl. Pap.* 1854,
I, p. 377.

[2] *Hansard*, 1855, CXXXIX, 1354-1369.

[3] *A Bill to Regulate the Hours of Labour of Females and Young Persons
under Eighteen employed in any of the Processes of Bleaching, etc. : Parl.
Pap.* 1856, I, p. 373.

[4] *Hansard* 1856, CXLIII, p. 210.

industry was the maximum of wisdom. Whilst fully admitting of course the duty which lay upon Parliament of ' protecting the health, the happiness, the comfort, and the well-being of the labouring classes ', he saw the bleaching trade exposed to the most severe competition with foreign rivals and the mistake that would be made by cramping and fettering it with legislation for the restriction of the hours of employment of children and of the age at which they should be employed.[1] Graham, supporting the Government in this matter, urged that the whole question should again be inquired into, this time by a Select Committee ; and in the end the Bill was once more defeated. Education, so far as children in bleach-works were concerned, had by this time taken a back place in the consideration of the legislators, and even the reference in the preamble to the Bill of 1854 to the expediency of giving opportunities for the education of the children had dropped out of the later Bills.

On 15th May, 1857, a Select Committee was appointed ' to inquire into the circumstances connected with the employment of women and children in the bleaching and dyeing establishments ', and the members met frequently during June and July. The evidence taken during those months from employers, operatives, clergymen, doctors and so on, was submitted to the House in the month of July, 1857.[2] But as the inquiry had not been completed by the end of the session, a further Committee was

---

[1] *Ibid.*, pp. 212-214.
[2] *First Report of the Select Committee on Bleaching and Dyeing Works, with Minutes of Evidence : Parl. Pap.* 1857, Sess. 2. I. *Second Report* : p. 261.

appointed early in 1858.[1] There was inevitably much conflict of evidence as between operatives and employers, in regard to the educational state of the children as well as to other matters. In the end, the Committee reported that whilst thinking that the circumstances connected with the employment of women and children in bleaching and dyeing were deserving of consideration, they were of opinion that employment in these industries should not be restricted by law.

Two years later, early in 1860, the parties interested in factory reform, nothing daunted by the set-back resulting from the Select Committee's report, promoted a further Bill.[2] On this occasion, however, it was for the first time proposed definitely to apply the provisions of the Factories Act to the employment of children in bleaching and dyeing works. An eloquent appeal by Roebuck, the member for Oldham and himself a large employer in the cotton industry, was mainly responsible for securing the second reading. It had been argued by one member that there was no analogy between the case of factories and that of bleaching and dyeing works. ' I do not care a straw,' said Roebuck, ' whether or not there is any analogy in this respect, but I am sure that there is an analogy in the suffering '. Referring to the evidence given in Tremenheere's report of a lad who had worked thirty-seven hours continuously, he continued, ' Now, I ask you, the gentlemen of England, if you will bear this. I hear great talk of humanity—lip humanity !—about the American slave . . . but I cannot

[1] *Report from the Select Committee on Bleaching and Dyeing Works, with Minutes of Evidence : Parl. Pap.* 1857-8, XI, p. 387.

[2] *A Bill to place the Employment of Women, Young Persons and Children in Bleaching Works and Dyeing Works under the Regulations of the Factories Acts : Parl. Pap.* 1860, I, p. 637.

help regarding with at least equal indignation the condition of the white slave of England. . . . The weak and the miserable appeal to you now for compassion and aid, and I, their humble advocate, also appeal to you in perfect confidence that you will listen to their prayer, and will pass this Measure for their relief.' That the House agreed to the second reading by 226 votes to 39 showed the effect of Roebuck's appeal. An amendment to exclude from the Bill employment in bleaching by the ' open air process ' was made before the third reading was given on 9th July and the Royal Assent on 6th August, 1860.[1] From 1st August, 1861, children employed in bleaching and dyeing were thus to become ' half-timers ' at school.

Reporting towards the end of 1861, Baker, the Factory Inspector in whose district Lancashire and Cheshire were situated, stated that there were 116 works in his district affected by the new Act. After a number of the children had been discharged as being under age, the number remaining in employment under the age of thirteen was 352 boys and 123 girls. Redgrave remarked that the number in his district was ' comparatively small ' and that the provisions respecting school attendance affected but few establishments. The Act, therefore, hard though the struggle had been to achieve it, did not in the event benefit any large number of children.

---

[1] 23/24 Vict., c. 78. It is of interest to note here that during the debate on the Bill Sir James Graham, who had so often been a formidable opponent of factory reform, recanted to some extent his former views. ' Experience had shown to his satisfaction that many of the predictions formerly made against the Factory Bill had not been verified by the result, and that, on the whole, that measure had contributed to the comfort and well-being of the working classes while it had not materially injured the masters'. House of Commons, 9 May, 1860. *Hansard* 1860, CLVIII, 984.

CHAPTER V

FURTHER EXTENSION OF LEGISLATION COLLIERIES AND MINES

THE Children's Employment Commission appointed in 1841 had been directed to inquire into the ' employment of children of the poorer classes in mines and collieries ' as well as in the various branches of trade and manufacture.[1] The Commissioners' *First Report*—which dealt with employment in mines and collieries—together with the reports from and evidence collected by the sub-commissioners who were appointed to make the inquiry in the various parts of the country, fill two large volumes of more than 1200 pages [2] The usual discrepancy as regards the actual conditions of employment was found between the statements of coal owners and managers and those of the workpeople themselves and also of many of the doctors, clergymen and schoolmasters. Although it was in general with extreme reluctance that witnesses of the former class would admit that children were employed even as early as seven years of age, yet the Commissioners found the evidence overwhelming that children were regularly at work at the age of five, six and seven.[3] These were mainly employed as

[1] *Cf. supra*, p. 108.

[2] *Children's Employment Commission : First Report of the Commissioners (Mines) : Parl. Pap.* 1842, XV, 1. *Appendix to First Report : Parl. Pap.* 1842, XVII, 1.

[3] *First Report*, p. 25.

air-door boys, or ' trappers,', ' fillers ', ' pushers ', and to drive horses. The ' trapper ' was commonly the youngest person employed in the mine and had charge of a door placed in a road, along which horses, men and boys were constantly passing, but through which it was essential to the ventilation of the mine to prevent the current of air from the shaft from passing. The trapper had the duty of opening the door for anyone who had occasion to pass through it, and then to shut it again as quickly as possible. On his doing this properly the safety of the mine depended. In the mines in which the seams of coal were too narrow and the roads too low for horses to go up to the working face, children called ' pushers ', commonly from ten to eleven years old, pushed the carriages either from the face to the horseways, or the whole distance to the foot of the shaft. In some districts, these children wore a harness consisting of a pair of leather straps over the shoulders, meeting in a broad piece behind and terminating in a chain and hook.[1] In others, ' a girdle is put round the naked waist, to which a chain from the carriage is hooked and passed between the legs, and the boys crawl on their hands and knees, drawing the carriage after them.'[2] In several, though not all, districts, children were employed in the manner described without distinction of sex ;[3] and in a large number of pits the men were accustomed to work in a state of perfect nakedness, assisted in their work ' by females of all ages, from girls of six years old to women of twenty-one, these females being themselves quite naked down to the waist '.[4] The hours of employment varied

[1] *Ibid*, pp. 78, 79.   [2] *Ibid.*, p. 79.
[3] e.g. Girls and women were not employed underground in South Staffordshire, Durham and Northumberland.
[4] *Ibid.*, p. 26.

from district to district. From Derbyshire, ' all classes of
witnesses concur in stating that . . . some of the children
and young persons work 16 hours out of the 24, reckoning
from the time they leave home in the morning until they
return home to it in the evening '.[1] Twelve hours a day,
however, were usual in many districts, though the children
were always absent from their homes at least thirteen
hours, and commonly more.[2] The population returns for
1841 had shown that nearly 90,000 persons were employed
in coal mining in England.[3] Of these, the Commissioners,
guided by returns they had received from many of the
colliery owners, estimated that about one-fifth—or 18,000
—were children, mostly boys, under thirteen years of age.[4]

As for the educational state of the children, the Commissioners described a state of neglect ' disgraceful to a
Christian country '.[5] From South Staffordshire, the
clergymen ' uniformly state that the means of instruction
are utterly inadequate to the wants of the people ; that
there is not provision for one-fourth of the uneducated
youth .' In the West Riding of Yorkshire ' almost the
only provision for the education of the colliery population
is Sunday schools '. In the neighbourhood of Halifax
the sub-commissioner found in an examination of 219
children and young persons in one of the coal-pits that only
31 could read an easy book, that not more than 15 could
write their names, and that ' the whole remaining number

---

[1] *Ibid.*, p. 106.

[2] *Cf.* Northumberland and Durham, *Ibid.*, p. 121.

[3] *Census Report for* 1841 (*Occupation Abstract*) : *Parl. Pap.* 1844, XXVII,
p. 38.

[4] *First Report*, p. 56. The proportion was greatest in Yorkshire and
least in Derbyshire.

[5] *Second Report* : *Parl. Pap.* 1843, XIII, 465-8.

were incapable of connecting two syllables together'. From the coal-fields of North Lancashire it was reported that education of the children had been almost wholly neglected—' their intellects are as little enlightened as their places of work—darkness reigns throughout'. In Cumberland ' the mental destitution in which the great body of collier children are growing up . . . is fearfully great ; they are as ignorant as it is well possible to conceive children to be.' ' With the exception of instruction received in Sunday schools, the most successful result of which is stated to be that they ' learn to put easy words together ', the collier children in [South Durham] receive no education of any kind whatever.' Where evening schools did exist, excessive fatigue after the long hours of their daily work rendered it almost out of the question for the colliery children to attend at all, certainly to attend with profit. From near Newcastle-upon-Tyne came the evidence of a schoolmaster that ' out of 100 boys down the pit, not more then ten will be at night-school in winter and none at all in summer. The boys on leaving the pit are sleepy, tired, and unfit for school, and nothing can be done for their learning while they are so long at work as at present. Pit parents never think of educating their children. . . . This is a private school, although the colliery owners built the school and master's house, and give the master coals every year. Each child 4d. for reading, 2d. more for writing, and 3d. for ciphering ; 10s. a quarter pays for everything. . . . There are but few pitmen's children here. . . . Two winters ago he had 30 boys at night school, of whom perhaps 20 were pit lads, and

L

these 20 always fell asleep.'[1]   Nor was ignorance the only characteristic of these children.   ' Throughout the whole district of the coal-field [West Riding of Yorkshire] the youthful population is in a state of profaneness and almost of mental imbecility.'   ' The ignorance and the degraded state of the colliers and their children [in Lancashire] are proverbial throughout this district.   They are uneducated, ignorant, and brutal ; deteriorated as workmen and danger-ous as subjects.'   Such were the reports of the sub-commissioners.

Fortified by the information which the Children's Employment Commission had made available, Lord Ashley very soon afterwards introduced a Bill[2] into the House of Commons, the main objects of which were to prohibit the employment in mines and collieries of all women and girls and of boys under the age of thirteen. Faced with opposition against so high an age being pre-scribed, Ashley agreed to alter it to ten years, with the proviso that up to the age of thirteen the children should work only three days in the week, every alternate day, and for not more than twelve hours a day.[3]   A clause was added authorising the appointment of inspectors, who should report to the Secretary of State on the state of the collieries and whether the provisions of the Act were being observed.   Although the Bill was supported in the Commons by a large colliery owner in Durham (Mr H.

---

[1] *Children's Employment Commission : Appendix to First Report : Parl. Pap.* 1842, XVI, p. 630.

[2] *A Bill to Prohibit the Employment of Women and Girls in Mines and Collieries, and to Regulate the Employment of Boys : Parl. Pap.* 1842, III. p. 275.   Introduced on 7th June, 1842.

[3] *Bill as Amended in Committee : Parl. Pap.* 1842, III, p. 283. *Hansard* 1842, LXIV, p. 426.

Lambton) on the ground that by preventing children from
going down the mines at a young age ' an infinity of good
in promoting the education of that population ' would be
achieved,[1] it was otherwise in the House of Lords. In the
view of the Marquis of Londonderry, the main spokesman
of the anti-reformers, who was also a large colliery owner
in the County of Durham, children were as fit for the work
at the age of eight as when they were ten. Moreover, if the
children were not employed before ten, how were the
colliers to bring up and educate them? In most cases the
parents were far too poor to pay for education.[2] They did
not seem to be aware, he said, that our fields could not be
ploughed, our mines wrought, nor our ships sailed by the
use of the pen alone. The requisite proportion of education
would always be supplied without making all this stir and
effort about it. If it should preponderate, the equilibrium
of society would be destroyed.[3] The valuable clause
restricting the number of days and the hours of employment of boys between the ages of ten and thirteen was
deleted, and the functions proposed for the inspectors were
narrowed. And in this form, prohibiting after 1st March,
1843, the employment underground of women and girls in
any case and that of boys under ten, the Bill was duly
passed.[4]

The Inspector, or Commissioner as he was termed,
appointed under the Act to supervise its working, was
Hugh Seymour Tremenheere.[5] By 1845 he found that
in eight of the large and in a few of the smaller collieries

[1] *Hansard* 1842, LXIII, p. 1354.
[2] *Hansard* 1842, LXV, p. 120.
[3] *Hansard* 1842, LXIV, pp. 543, 544.
[4] 5 and 6 Vict. c. 99.
[5] Appointed on 28th November, 1843 : *Parl. Pap.* 1844, XVI, p. 3.

in the West Riding of Yorkshire, specific efforts had been
made by the proprietors for the education and general
benefit of their employees ; but there were very numerous
places, ' many dark spots ', where little or nothing had been
attempted.[1] In Northumberland and Durham there were
several schools, established by colliery owners and under
competent masters ; but very few of the colliers' children
attended them—in one school only 12 out of 60 scholars,
and in another six out of 50.   Sometimes there were schools
' of the old kind . . . kept by men of their own class ' ;
and often, even where new schools under trained teachers,
charging lower fees (1d. or 2d. per week) were available, the
colliers preferred to send their children to the schools of
the former type.[2] Consett Iron and Coal Company
(Durham) stood almost alone in the thoroughness of its
interest and provision for the education of the children.
By 1849 the proprietors had established almost a complete
school system, of eight schools—two boys' and one girls'
attached to the Established Church, and four boys' and
one girls' attached to Nonconformist Churches.   The
masters of these schools were paid £70 to £80 a year and
provided with a house.   A sum of 1d. per week was
deducted from the wages of the employees, and the remaining sum required for the schools was paid by the company.
' The children are admitted to each school by printed
orders issued by one of the agents.   If any child is absent
he is reported, and inquiry is directly made of the parents
as to the cause.   For the 1d. per week, all the children of
a family are admitted.'[3]   In the colliery district of South

[1] *Report of the Mining Commissioner :* 1845, XXVII, pp. 217, 235.

[2] *Report of the Mining Commissioner : Parl. Pap.* 1846, XXIV. p. 395.

[3] *Report of the Mining Commissioner : Parl. Pap.* 1849, XXII, pp. 401,
402.

Staffordshire, however, there was little progress to be observed. Mainly, doubtless, this was due to lack of interest and help from the employers.[1] But partly also it was due to the mere cupidity and selfishness of the parents, who were too ready to remove their children from school as soon as they could earn a shilling or two a week. Frequently, Tremenheere wrote, the parents were in the habit of urging the schoolmasters to ' finish their boys quickly ' that they might be put to work—by which expression was meant ' only a little reading, a very little ciphering, and the power of reading, however imperfectly.'[2] In his report of 1850, Tremenheere expressed the hope that, if public opinion in the mining districts was not yet prepared for an amendment of the law, employers would themselves voluntarily ' adopt the principle of the Factories and the Printworks Acts in the subject of the education of the children '.[3] In some parts, however, more especially in Northumberland and Durham, opinion appeared to be forming in the desired way. In 1847, a petition, promoted by the ' Miners' Association ', which claimed to speak for 60,000 colliers, had been addressed to the House of Commons, and one of its principal objects had been to induce Parliament to apply the educational clauses of the Factory Acts to the mining districts.[4] In Northumberland and Durham at least, Tremenheere had at the same period found the owners and managers, without exception, most ready and willing to second these views.[5] In 1851 ' several

[1] *Report of the Mining Commissioner :* Parl. Pap. 1850, XXIII, pp. 599, 600.
[2] *Report of the Mining Commissioner :* Parl. Pap. 1851, XXIII, p. 452.
[3] *Report of the Mining Commissioner :* Parl. Pap. 1850, XXIII, p. 600.
[4] *Report of the Mining Commissioner :* Parl. Pap. 1847, XVI, p. 409.
[5] *Ibid.,* p. 407.

gentlemen, very prominently interested in the welfare and
improvement of the colliery population' of these two
counties, had communicated to Tremenheere a proposition
that steps should be taken by Parliament to raise the age
of employment to twelve and to make attendance at school
on two days a week compulsory on all boys employed
between twelve and fifteen years of age.[1] To go so far,
however, was more than the Commissioner was prepared
to recommend. Instead, he thought, the precedent of the
Printworks Act was more suitable, and he accordingly
urged the adoption of a provision whereby all boys between
ten and fourteen in the collieries should be compelled to
attend school for 'thirty days of 150 hours in every six
months' (the words of the Printworks Act).[2] Nor would
it have been inconvenient to arrange for this. It was the
habit of at least three-quarters of the whole of the collieries
in the country to be idle every alternate Monday, or even
every Monday. On these days therefore the boys employed
were also necessarily idle ; and nothing would be easier,
represented Tremenheere, than that they should go to
school. With six hours' attendance at a school on every
Monday, the half-yearly amount of 150 hours' schooling
suggested would be obtained. Even if attendance were
on alternate Mondays only, the remaining hours might,
if evening schools were extended, be made up by evening
attendance.[3] Even provision compelling attendance at
school for 100 hours every half year, ' made up by an
attendance at the night school on two evenings per week
for two hours each evening, or by occasional attendance

[1] *Report of Mining Commissioner : Parl. Pap.* 1852, XXI, p. 458.
[2] *Ibid.,* pp. 459, 460.
[3] *Report of Mining Commissioner : Parl. Pap.* 1852-53, XL, p. 576.

at the day school, on days when they were not employed below ground ', would be of essential service to the boys and the community.[1]

Nor was the appointment of a single Commissioner, with very limited powers, sufficient to ensure that the law relating to the age of employment was obeyed. Unlike the Factories Act, there were no arrangements for certificates of age being required, nor for the keeping of registers by colliery owners to provide information concerning the children employed. So far as the employment of children was concerned, Tremenheere was charged alone with the duty of visiting the colliery owners in the whole of the United Kingdom.[2] The only means he could adopt was to employ from time to time a constable to watch a certain colliery where there was reason to believe that the Act was not complied with, and, if satisfactory evidence was produced, to prosecute the offenders. It is hardly surprising therefore that he had to report in 1852, ten years after the Act was passed, that it was notorious that boys under ten were continually at work;[3] and again, a few years later, that in this regard non-compliance with the law was on the increase.[4] Tremenheere's last report as a Commissioner under the Mining Act was made in 1859.[5]

---

[1] *Report of Mining Commissioner : Parl. Pap.* 1856, XVIII, p. 564.

[2] Several Inspectors of Mines were appointed on the passing of the Coal Mines Act, 1850, to inquire into and report on the safety of mines.

[3] *Ibid.*, p. 574.

[4] *Report of Mining Commissioner : Parl. Pap.* 1854-5, XV, p. 562.

[5] The Mines Act of the following year consolidated the provisions for the restriction of the employment of children in mines with other provisions dealing with safety and the prevention of accidents generally ; and the duty of supervising the working of the Act as a whole was placed on the Inspectors of Mines

For more than fifteen years he had been unfailing in his annual reports in urging with force and conviction the great need of mending the appalling state of ignorance among the colliery population. ' Are the mass of boys destined to colliery labour now receiving that instruction, and are they subjected to that amount of mental and moral training, which affords a reasonable expectation that they will form, when they grow up, a more enlightened class than those who have gone before them ? I regret to say that [they] are not. . . . When they leave school, at or about the age of ten, when they go down into the pits . . . they may be said to have learnt scarcely anything to any good purpose. . . . If any real improvement in the intelligence of the colliery population is to be looked for within any reasonable time, recourse must be had to legislation. . . ."[1]

Accidents in coal mines, often involving serious loss of life, and also disablement to many, had for many years been frequent.[2] Parliament was accordingly moved in 1850 to appoint Inspectors of Coal Mines, charged with the duty of inspecting collieries as to ventilation, lighting and safety generally[3]; and to extend their duties and powers by a further Act[4] passed in 1855.[5] Though lack

[1] *Report of Mining Commissioner : Parl. Pap.* 1859, Sess. 2, XII, p. 465.

[2] *Cf. Report of the Select Committee on Accidents in Mines : Parl. Pap.* 1835, V, 1. *First Report of the Midland Mines Commission : Parl. Pap,* 1843, XIII, 1. *Report of the House of Lords on Accidents : Parl. Pap.* 1849, VII, 1. *Report of Select Committee on Coal Mines : Parl. Pap.* 1852, V, 1.

[3] 13 and 14 Vict., c. 100.

[4] 18 and 19 Vict., c. 109.

[5] The number of inspectors appointed at first was quite inadequate. *Cf. :* ' The number of collieries in England and Wales was at that time, 1851, estimated at 1,200, so that to examine every colliery once a year every inspector would have to visit 300 mines—a labour practically impossible. , . . When the reports of the inspectors for the year were published, it

of safety devices and precautions, for which the colliery
owners and their managers might be held largely responsible,
had doubtless been the main cause of the great loss of life
and of health, some part of it could be attributed to the
ignorance and lack of education of the miners themselves
and to the employment of very young children.[1] 'Do
you not think,' a Staffordshire colliery manager was asked
by the Select Committee on Accidents in Mines in 1835,
'it would be expedient to place a printed list with a few
simple rules of instruction in their hands ? ' ' Most of
them,' he replied, ' are men that could not read '.[2] ' I
should say a very inconsiderable proportion of the grown-up
pitmen can read ', was the reply of a Durham colliery
manager to a similar question.[3] Accordingly, the Mines
Inspectors appointed in 1850 were informed that although
' it will not fall within your province to take any direct
measures for promoting education among the miners, you
may usefully avail yourself of any fitting opportunity of
pointing out to them its importance and advantages, and
lend your influence to the encouragement of any well-

was found that in 1851 the number of recorded deaths through accidents
at collieries amounted to 1,062, this being the first truthful record of lives
lost in collieries for any definite period.' *Coal Mines Inspection*,
Boyd, R. N. (1879), pp. 108-9.

[1] ' A great source of danger in mines, in addition to the inhumanity of
the practice, is the employment of boys of a very early age, much under
10 years, whence have arisen explosions and accidents of a very serious
nature . . . When Willingdon Pit " fired " and destroyed 32 human
beings, it was given in evidence at the coroner's inquest, that it was caused
by a boy nine years old, a trapper named Richard Cooper, who had left
his door open to go and play with another little boy who had charge of the
adjoining door '. Report of the South Shields Committee on Accidents
in Coal Mines, given as *Appendix* 4 *of Report of Select Committee on Coal
Mines : Parl. Pap.* 1852, V, 229.

[2] *Select Committee on Accidents in Mines : Parl. Pap.* 1835, V, p. 215.

[3] *Ibid.*, p. 92.

devised plans for advancing their moral and intellectual improvement '.[1] That the Inspectors of Mines did so is clear from the occasional details concerning their efforts in the matter given in their annual reports. ' The want of education amongst the foremen and deputies is the most serious drawback with which I have to contend,' wrote one inspector concerning the prevention of accidents, ' and the amendment of this involves a much more general system of education. But a small proportion of colliers and deputies can read and write : and this fact I have constantly pressed on the attention of the coalowners '.[2] ' The subject of education is forcing itself on the attention of all classes of the community,' wrote another inspector in 1858 ; ' but the subject that seems to baffle the good intentions of those actually engaged in this benevolent object seems to be the difficulty of keeping children long enough at school, to make what they learn sink deep on the mind, so as to make a lasting impression.' In face of this difficulty his hope that they might ' be induced to remain at school until they are fifteen years of age '[3] must

[1] *Instructions addressed to the Inspectors of Coal Mines : Parl. Pap.* 1851, XLIII, pp. 401, 402.

[2] *Reports of Inspectors of Coal Mines : Parl. Pap.* 1854, XIX, p. 795.

[3] *Reports of the Inspectors of Coal Mines : Parl. Pap.* 1857-58, XXXII, p. 84. This inspector was also rather in advance of the time in his ideas as to a ' practical bias ' being given to the education of the older children. ' It is the practice of school committees ', he wrote, ' to appeal to manufacturers to give a preference to such boys as remain to obtain a prize ; but why should they do so ? There is nothing taught that will make him more forward in the branch of mechanics or other skilled labour he may select ; he may be better fitted for a clerk, and much better fitted to fulfil the duties of manhood, but as a miner, a furnaceman, a puddler, or any other industrious occupation, he is not improved in the slightest degree . . . What I think ought to be adopted, is a more useful education—something that shall fit the boy to become a clever man as well as a good one—that whilst he is improving his moral perceptions, he should acquire some knowledge of using his mental and physical powers to advantage.'

be described as the height of optimism. 'The necessity of educating the working classes,' reported yet another inspector in 1859, ' becomes more evident every day. To adult persons I do not particularly refer ; as regards them, it would I fear be a hopeless task, beyond that of moral training and strict discipline. It is the cause of the rising generation which I am advocating, of those who will have to manage and work deeper shafts, surrounded by greater dangers than any that have yet been reached and perhaps seen ; and hence arises the question how and by what means are such desirable results to be obtained ? . . . While it affords some relief to find in many places in the mining districts a system of general education may be obtained,[1] it disappears like a dissolving view ; on dis-covering that as it is not compulsory, it is too frequently neglected.'[2]

Parliament was accordingly induced to take the matter into consideration, and a Government Bill was introduced on the 14th February, 1860.[3] The Bill proposed that no boy under twelve should be employed in mines, except that a boy between ten and twelve might be employed on condition first, that before being employed he was certified

---

[1] e.g. ' The rapid extension of the means of popular education in the South Staffordshire mining district, appears in the fact that within this district, comprising about 200,000 people, and occupying an area of about ten miles square, there have been built in the last ten or twelve years thirty new schools, capable of accommodating about 8,000 children, nearly all of them being now under certificated teachers, with apprentices, and annual grants in aid of their support from the parliamentary fund.' Rev. J. P. Norris, H.M.I., in *Transactions of the National Association for the Promotion of Social Science*, 1858, p. 293.

[2] *Report of Inspectors of Coal Mines : Parl. Pap.* 1859, Sess. 2, XII, p. 345.

[3] *A Bill for the Regulation and Inspection of Mines : Parl. Pap.* 1860, IV, pp. 745, 759, 773, 789.

' under the hand of a competent schoolmaster ' to be able
to read and write, and secondly, that while employed a
similar certificate was obtained by the mine owner every
month showing that the boy had attended school for not
less than twenty hours during the month preceding.   No
proposal to limit the number of hours of employment was
included, and indeed amendments to make illegal the
employment of a boy between ten and fourteen for more
than eight hours, and even ten hours, in any one day, were
defeated.[1]   An unsuccessful effort was also made to raise
the age of exclusion, subject to the educational provisions,
from twelve to thirteen years, with the view of bringing
colliery employment into line in this respect with employment in textile factories.[2]   And though an effort to provide
for the attendance at school of children between ten and
twelve to be for five hours on each of two days a week was
defeated, in the end some improvement in this respect was
achieved by the provision that the attendance should be
for not less than three hours a day for two days in the
week.   In this form, then, the Act[3] was passed—children
under ten to be excluded from employment, as heretofore ;
and employment between the ages of ten and twelve
(without restriction of hours) to be limited to children who
were certified before being employed as being able to read
and write and in respect of whom monthly certificates were

[1] *Hansard* 1860, CLIX, pp. 409-413 ; *ibid.*, 845-850.

[2] It is of interest to note that the mover of this amendment, Mr Paget,
had been an opponent of the earlier Factory Bills.   He was now, however,
' convinced from the experience he had had of its working that its educational clauses had conferred great benefit on the operatives, both mentally,
morally, and physically, and he had never met with any person who did
not concur in that statement.'   *Hansard* 1860, CLIX, p. 397.

[3] 23 and 24 Vict., c. 151.

obtained by the mine owner showing that attendance at school had been made for three hours a day on two days a week during the month preceding. The Act (the provisions of which came into effect on 1st July, 1861) extended to iron mines as well as coal mines. The inspectors appointed under the Act were charged with the duty of inquiring into and reporting on whether the provisions of the Act were complied with.

The new law, so far as the employment of boys was concerned, was not met with any enthusiasm in the colliery districts. The education of boys under the age of twelve years raised a loud outcry both from colliers and their agents, it was reported from Lancashire in 1863.[1] Refusal on the part of the owners to employ boys under twelve soon became common, and even general,[2] ' and by this

[1] *Reports of Inspectors of Mines for* 1863 : *Parl. Pap.* 1864, XXIV, Pt. I, p. 79.

[2] *Ibid.*, pp. 79, 91 : The Inspector for South Staffordshire and Worcestershire found during the year 1863 only one boy employed between the ages of 10 and 12 years. In the following year the Inspector for the Northern District reported that ' scarcely any boys . . . either above ground or below ' were then employed. *Parl. Pap.* 1865, XX, p. 611. *Cf.* also : ' Wherever I have had the opportunity, in colliery schools, I have inquired whether the Mines Regulations Act of 1860 has had any perceptible influence in raising the age of scholars' attendance, i.e. in promoting the attendance of boys between 10 and 12. The answer, both from the schoolmasters and from owners or viewers, has, I believe, invariably been in the negative. I believe the provisions of the Act are fairly carried out, but I am not aware of any instances of boys attending school and receiving the certificate required. Viewers would rather dispense with them altogether than have the trouble of looking after the certificates. It does not, however, I am sorry to say, follow that because they do not go down the pit they are therefore at school. Other employment, not within the scope of the Act, is found for them, so that nothing is commoner than to be assured on good authority on the one hand, that there are no boys of that age in the pit, and to see on the other hand that there are hardly any of them at school.' *Report of the Committee of Council on Education,* 1863-64 (*Rev. G. R. Moncrieff's Report*—Northumberland, Durham, and Cumberland) : *Parl. Pap.* 1864, XLV, p. 105.

means the owners relieve themselves of the responsibility of attending to certificates.'[1] Schoolmasters, by reminding the owners and managers in cases where there was any suspicion that boys were employed contrary to the Act, often assisted materially in the administration of the law.[2] ' But a very general feeling prevails that if such a measure is necessary for mines, it is equally applicable to large manufacturing interests ', remarked one of the inspectors ;[3] another inspector adding that while the great demand for child labour at a high rate of wages in trades ' where ignorance is permitted ' continued, he feared that the majority of future pit boys would still grow up into manhood as uneducated as before the educational clauses of the Mines Act were enacted.[4] Though doubtless substantially true, this was perhaps a too gloomy view of the situation.   More schools were certainly being erected in most colliery districts, many of the chief collieries either possessing schools of their own or their owners contributing to the support of neighbouring schools.[5] ' I was employed ', Mr Peter Higson, Inspector of Mines in the West Lancashire and North Wales District, wrote in 1867, ' in the erection of, I believe, the first school in Lancashire, that was provided expressly for the education of the children of miners.   It was built at Clifton, near Manchester, in the year 1836, at the expense of the trustees of the late Ellis Fletcher, Esquire, whose mines I then managed.   The number of schools that have been since built and established, and the

---

[1] *Reports of Inspectors of Mines : Parl. Pap.* 1865, **XX**, p. 666.
[2] *Reports of Inspectors of Mines : Parl. Pap.* 1864, **XXIV**, Part I, p. 91.
[3] *Ibid.,* p. 103.
[4] *Ibid.,* p. 129.
[5] *Reports of Inspectors of Mines : Parl. Pap.* 1865, **XX**, pp. 611, 634.

number of children that daily attend them, are too numerous to mention here. . . .'

Before 1870, therefore, the employment of boys under twelve in mines had almost entirely ceased throughout the country ; and in the very rare instances where boys under this age were employed, it was mostly where the mother was a widow, or the family large or in unusually poor circumstances.[1]

Early in 1869, the Home Secretary, Mr H. A. Bruce, introduced a Bill[2] to consolidate and amend the Mines Acts. The main objects of this Bill were to make provision for greater safety and for the prevention of accidents, which had continued to be all too frequent occurrences, the average loss of life being then about 1,000 lives a year.[3] Included in the Bill were clauses (1) to prohibit the employment of children under the age of twelve years below ground in any coal or iron mine, (2) to limit boys between the ages of twelve and thirteen and male young persons up to sixteen years employed below ground to a maximum of twelve hours' employment a day, and (3) to extend to children and young persons employed above ground the provisions of the Workshops Regulation Act 1867.[4] As it was not found practicable to make progress with the Bill

---

[1] *Report of Inspectors of Mines : Parl. Pap.* 1868-9, XIV, p. 624. See also *Report of Select Committee on Mines : Parl. Pap.* 1865, XII, p. 605 ; 1866, XIV, p. 1 ; 1867, XII, p. 1. This Report contains the Minutes of a very thorough inquiry into the matter, including the state of education of children in mines, the provision and conduct of schools in connection with mines, suggestions by witnesses for increased educational facilities, etc.

[2] *Bill to Consolidate and Amend the Acts relating to the Regulation and Inspection of Mines : Parl. Pap.* 1868-9, IV, p. 79.

[3] *Hansard* 1870, CXCIX, p. 595.

[4] *Cf. infra*, p. 201.

in that year, a further Bill on the same lines[1] was introduced by Mr Bruce on 10th February, 1870. The reception of the measure was very different from what had been shown to former Bills on the subject. The conscience of the country seemed to have been aroused by the repeated accounts, made by the inspectors year by year, of the lack of safety precautions in mines, and the dreadful toll of life and the absence of care for the well-being of both adults and children. Mr Bruce adopted an attitude almost of apology for the absence from the Bill of specific provisions for the education of the colliery children.[2] The existing provisions (of the Act of 1860) were, he recognised, totally inadequate to secure the education of the children. There was, for example, no security that the certificate required in respect of boys between ten and twelve would be given by a competent person, such as the master of a school inspected by the Inspector of Schools under the Education Department. Though it was required under the Act of 1860 that children before being employed should be able to read and write, he went on to say, no definition of proficiency in reading and writing was given—the very slightest capacity to read and write would satisfy the terms of the Act. He relied, however, on the Education Bill which had recently been brought forward by Mr W. E. Forster becoming law, thus ensuring the attendance of children at school and the provision by the locally elected school boards of an adequate number of schools to accommodate them.

[1] *A Bill to Consolidate and Amend the Acts relating to the Regulation and Inspection of Mines : Parl. Pap.* 1870, III, pp. 441, 465. This Bill provided for the twelve hours of employment in the case of young persons being inclusive of one and a half hours for meals.

[2] *Hansard* 1870, CXCIX, pp. 594-608.

The immediate progress of the measure was, however, retarded by another consideration. Some years earlier, a Royal Commission had been appointed to inquire into the condition (including the employment of children) of all mines to which the Mines Act of 1860 did not apply, i.e. to mines other than coal and iron mines.[1] One of the recommendations of the Commission had been that, as a general rule, no boys under the age of fourteen years should be permitted to work below the surface.[2] In February 1870, a few days after Mr Bruce had introduced his Mines Bill, Lord Kinnaird, who had been Chairman of the Royal Commission of 1862, notified the House, that as the Government had taken no action on the Commission's Report and as there was a strong case for legislation, he himself would introduce a measure. Two months later, urgent representation that mines other than coal and iron mines should be included within the scope of the Mines Bill, combined with the effect of a recent deplorable accident in some shale mines, induced Mr Bruce to adopt this proposal Pressure of business, however, prevented the matter from being dealt with by Parliament that year. When in February 1871 the new Bill[3] was introduced, it was seen that some changes in the measure, so far as children were concerned, had been made. It was now proposed that the minimum age of employment should be maintained at ten years (as it had been under the Act of 1860), and not raised to twelve as had been proposed in the Bill of the preceding year. Between the ages of ten and

[1] *Copy of Royal Commission on Mines : Parl. Pap.* 1862, LV, p. 775.
[2] *Report of the Commissioners : Parl. Pap.* 1864, XXIV, Part I, p. 532.
[3] *A Bill to Consolidate and Amend the Acts relating to the Regulation of Mines : Parl. Pap.* 1871, IV, p. 229.

M

thirteen no boy was to be permitted to be employed below ground for more than three days a week or for more than twelve hours in any one day ; and for boys between thirteen and sixteen the maximum weekly number of hours was to be fifty-six. Boys between ten and thirteen were to attend school for at least ten hours a week, a certificate from the principal teacher of the school attended being required weekly. The mine owner would deduct a sum not exceeding 2d. per week from the boy's wages for payment to the schoolmaster.

These proposals, opposed as they were, in regard to the employment of boys below twelve years of age, to the recommendations of the Royal Commission, clearly demanded some explanation. The Association of Miners had put forward proposals that not only should a boy be refused employment before twelve but also a certain standard of proficiency in reading, writing and arithmetic should be required as a condition of employment. In this, Mr Bruce saw something more than a desire for education, saw indeed a desire to prevent the employment of children in order to keep up the rate of wages, and this object therefore must be opposed.[1] Encountering opposition in subsequent discussion, on the ground that different require-ments were needed for coal and iron mines and for metalli-ferous mines, he agreed to go back on his resolution to combine the two classes of mines.[2] A fresh Bill[3] was accordingly introduced in May 1871 to deal with metal-liferous mines, and the original Bill was amended so that

[1] *Hansard* 1871, CCIV, p. 195.   [2] *Hansard* 1871, CCV, p. 1770.

[3] *Bill to Amend the Law relating to the Regulation of Mines other than Coal Mines : Parl. Pap.* 1871, IV, 1. *Bill to Consolidate and Amend the Acts relating to the Regulating of Coal Mines (as amended in Committee) : Parl. Pap.* 1871, IV, p. 261.

it should apply only to coal and iron mines. The provisions, however, as to the age of employment of children and as to their education between the ages of ten and thirteen remained ; but faced once more with the pressure of business in Parliament, the Home Secretary had to abandon the measures for that session. At length, in 1872, the two Acts were passed, applicable in England from 1st January, 1873—the first applying to coal, iron, and shale mines,[1] the second to all other mines of whatever description.[2] The main part of these Acts consisted of provisions calculated to provide for the safety and proper discipline of the persons employed in mines and to prevent accidents. The provisions concerning children were not precisely the same in these two measures.

Under the Coal Mines Act:

(1) No child under ten years of age could be employed either above or below ground ;

(2) A boy between the age of ten and twelve could, on permission of the Secretary of State being given, be employed below ground in a mine where the thinness of the seams justified it. In this case, the employment was restricted as to days and hours ;

(3) A boy between twelve and sixteen[3] could not be employed for more than ten hours a day or for more than fifty-four hours a week ;

(4) A boy between the ages of ten and twelve must attend school for at least twenty-four hours in every two weeks during which he was employed, weekly certificates of school attendance being obtained by the employer from the principal teacher of the school.

---

[1] 35 and 36 Vict., c. 76.   [2] 35 and 36 Vict., c. 77.
[3] From the age of thirteen termed a ' young person '.

The employer was empowered to deduct a sum not exceeding 2*d*. per week from the boy's wages for payment to the
master of the school.   The Inspectors of Mines were given
authority to disqualify from granting certificates any
teacher who was deemed unfit because of ignorance, or
neglect, or lack of necessary books and materials in the
school, or because of immoral conduct or of neglect to fill
up proper certificates.   The provisions of the Act regarding
the boys between ten and twelve and regarding young persons
under sixteen applied also to employment above ground.

The Metalliferous Mines Act, on the other hand, prohibited the employment below ground of children under
twelve years of age and all women and girls, and limited,
as in the case of the Coal Mines Act, the employment below
ground of boys between twelve and thirteen and ' male
young persons ' between thirteen and sixteen to fifty-four
hours per week and ten hours in any one day.   No regulations regarding the education of boys were included.

The Acts, so far as the provisions regarding children
were concerned, appeared at once to be very generally
complied with.   In one or two districts, advantage was
taken of the rule that boys between ten and twelve might
be employed in mines where the seams were thin ;[1] but
this relatively small number apart, the inspectors reported
uniformly that practically no boys under twelve were
anywhere employed in mines.

---

[1] *Reports of Inspectors of Mines : Parl. Pap.* 1875, XVI, p. 740.   In the
Yorkshire and Lincolnshire district the number of these children was 615
in 1874, and 470 in 1875, and in the North and East Lancashire district
278 in 1874 ; but this was exceptional.   In the latter year, e.g., no boy
under 12 was employed underground, and only 23 boys and eight girls
under 13 years, above ground, in North Staffordshire, Cheshire, and Shrop-
shire district.

CHAPTER VI

AGRICULTURE

THE employment of children in agriculture and their opportunities for receiving education had come under investigation from time to time from the thirties onwards. The subject had been mentioned in 1834, though only incidentally, in connection with the work of the 'Select Committee on the Education of the Poorer Classes'. 'Do you think it would be advantageous for children in agricultural parishes to be entirely kept away from their agricultural labour for the purpose of attending schools ? ' the treasurer of the British and Foreign School Society had been asked. ' I think it decidedly,' he had replied, though adding that two or three years of instruction would be enough.[1] In 1842, four assistant commissioners were specially appointed to make a report to the Poor Law Commission on the employment of women and children in agriculture. ' The Commissioners desire,' the Secretary, Edwin Chadwick, informed them, ' that your main attention should be directed to the employment of children ; and that you will particularly inquire into the ages at which they begin to work, and the effects which their occupation or labour may produce upon their bodily health, as well as upon their opportunity for obtaining

[1] *Report from the Select Committee on the State of Education : Parl. Pap.* 1834, IX, p. 84.

167

school instruction and moral and religious education '.[1]
The report of the Assistant Commissioner who visited
Wilts, Dorset, Devon and Somerset gives a picture which
is perhaps a fair sample of what was found to be the state
of affairs over most of the country districts in 1842 :—

' I should say that, in the greater number of agricultural parishes there are day schools, which a considerable
number of the children of both sexes of the labouring
classes attend. Children go to these schools at the age
of five, six, or seven years. . . . Reading and writing,
and sometimes a little arithmetic, are taught ; to which,
occasionally, some other occupation is added. . . . I
found that in 34 schools in agricultural parishes the
average age of the youngest children in the first class
of the school was $9\frac{3}{4}$; and that the average age of the
eldest children in such class was $12\frac{1}{4}$. The instruction
of children who have not reached the first class rarely
includes writing.

' The age at which boys first go out to farm-labour
varies from seven to twelve, the ordinary age, where
they go to school, being between ten and eleven. Many
are taken from school to go to work before they have
reached the best class, and the majority of them soon
after they have reached it. Boys taken from school to
be put out to farm labour can generally read, sometimes
correctly ; but they cannot often write with sufficient
ease for useful purposes. . . . It also generally happens
when boys remain at the day school later than the age
of seven or eight, that, until they are finally taken away,
they go out to work in the fields at particular seasons of

[1] *Reports on the Employment of Women and Children in Agriculture :
Parl. Pap.* 1843, XII, xv.

the year. . Girls are also, but much more rarely than boys, taken away from the day school to work. . . . The effect of these interruptions in the attendance of children at school is frequently mischievous, as far as their progress is concerned. . . . Upon the whole, there can be no doubt that the employment of children in agriculture deprives them of opportunities of instruction both moral and religious, as well as of ordinary school instruction.'[1]

Inevitably there was not perfect uniformity in this respect throughout the country. Of education in the agricultural parts of Yorkshire, e.g., it was reported that ' while this matter is improving rather than the reverse . . . its general condition is anything but good. . . . It is very discreditable to the country that so large a proportion of its inhabitants should be left, as they are left, in profound ignorance. . . . School, as might be supposed, is invariably sacrificed to work '.[2] On the other hand, it was found that ' the education in Northumberland is very good ; and the people are intelligent and acute, alive to the advantages of knowledge, and eager to acquire it ; it is a rare thing to find a grown-up labourer who cannot read and write, and who is not capable of keeping his own accounts '.[3]

[1] *Report on the Employment of Women and Children in Agriculture :* Parl. Pap. 1843, XII, p. 36 *et seq.*

[2] *Ibid.*, pp. 291-293.

[3] *Ibid.*, p. 300. *Cf.* also the following extract quoted by the Assistant Commissioner from a ' pamphlet lately published by Mr Grey, of Dilston, on the subject of Agriculture in Northumberland ' : ' In contrasting the condition of the peasantry in the southern with those of the northern parts of the Kingdom, it would be highly improper to pass over unnoticed the superior education of the latter, and the effect which is produced by it upon their worldly circumstances, as well as upon their moral and religious

There was thus, in general, throughout the rural areas a fair provision of schools—not, of course, everywhere, nor in all cases affording sufficient accommodation or an efficient education ; and it was the common custom for the majority of the children of agricultural workers to attend them, though with imperfect regularity, for a few years before the age of ten.

The accounts of education in agricultural districts given by the Assistant Commissioner who inquired into ' the state of popular education in England ' for the Education Commission of 1858 show that by the latter year little, if any, progress had been made. In a large area of the East Midlands it was found that in 643 schools, only 14 per cent. of the boys were aged eleven years or more.[1] Boys and girls still began to leave school finally as early as nine ; and even before this age absences from school, as had been found to be the case nearly 20 years before, were long and frequent by reason of the children being able to earn wages. ' Children begin to have a money value as soon as they can shout loud enough to scare a crow, or can endure exposure to the weather in watching cows in the lane.'[2] While nominally attending school they were commonly kept at home to assist in any or all of the ' seven annual harvests . . . bark-peeling, hay, corn, hops, potatoes, apples,

education. No greater stigma can attach to parents than that of leaving their children without the means of education, and every nerve is strained to procure it. In the school attached to almost every village, one finds children not only able to read and write at a very early age, but most expert in all the common rules of arithmetic, and not infrequently capable of extracting the square and cube root with great expedition and accuracy ; and even the young men who labour in the fields all the day often spend a couple of hours in the evening in school, to advance themselves in such acquirements '. *Ibid.*, p. 302.

[1] Education Commission : *Reports of Assistant Commissioners : Parl. Pap.* 1861, XXI, Part II. *Rev. Thomas Hedley's Report*, p. 169.

[2] *Ibid.*, p. 147.

acorns. Add to these, bird-keeping in autumn and spring, potato-setting, hop-tying, and the incidental duties of baby-nursing and errand going ',[1] and the evil of the sporadic and irregular school attendance of the time is readily explained.

' I have asked many persons interested in the education of the poor [in agricultural districts] whether they would like to see any system of half-time attendance enforced by legislative enactment, but I have found very little feeling in favour of such a thing,' reported one of the Assistant Commissioners.[2] Doubtless the fact that many of the children would have had a long distance to go to school might have made a half-day system impracticable in country districts ; but an alternate day or alternate week system could hardly have been open to the same objections, a view which was urged in Parliament in 1867 by Mr. H. Fawcett.[3] On this occasion, the Government put the matter off by stating that the question of children employed in agriculture had not so far been dealt with by the Children's Employment Commission (which had been conducting investigations since 1862), though so far as employment in ' Agricultural gangs ' was concerned the Commission had the matter in hand.[4] The Report of the

[1] *Rev. James Fraser's Report : ibid.*, p. 26.

[2] *Rev. Thomas Hedley : ibid.*, p. 153. *Cf.* also, for an opposite view, *Communications from Edwin Chadwick, Esq., C.B., Relative to Education*, including ' On the Half-time School System as applied to Agricultural Employment. C. Paget, Esq., M.P.' : *Parl. Pap.* 1862, XLIII, p. 40.

[3] *Hansard* 1867, CLXXXV, p. 1069, Fawcett moved ' That in the opinion of this House, it is expedient to extend the Educational Clauses of the Factory Acts to children who are employed in agriculture.'

[3] *Hansard* 1867, CLXXXV, p. 1085. ' I will frankly add that . . . I have arrived at the conclusion that some of the principles of the Factory Acts will have to be extended to the agricultural districts . . . what the form may be I do not now say." Spencer Walpole (Home Secretary).

Commission was issued soon after,[1] its scope, however, being limited mainly to children employed in ' gangs ', a system which was peculiar to the eastern counties. For these the Commissioners stated that it would be desirable to require that all children working in ' gangs ' should, previously to being engaged by the gangmaster, produce a certificate from a schoolmaster that they had attended school for a certain number of hours ' somewhat according to the principle of the Act . . . called the Printworks Regulation Act, 1847 '.[2] It was, however, the Report stated, undoubtedly important that the school attendance should be distributed as regularly as possible, and that a more definite arrangement should be adopted than that of the Printworks Act. Finally, the Commissioners reported, their inquiry had also incidentally called attention to the large number of children in the districts investigated ' who, although not employed in gangs, are taken at the earliest possible age (between six and seven years and upwards) to work in some department or other of agricultural labour ; from which period their opportunities of school attendance almost entirely cease. . . . It would appear that these latter children, as well as those employed in gangs, equally demand the attention of the State, and are in as much need . . . of some legislative measure for their protection from an unreasonable amount of work, and for their education '.[3] The Report, with the abundance of evidence it produced to justify its statements, clearly

---

[1] Children's Employment Commission (1862) : *Sixth Report, Parl. Pap.* 1867, XVI, p. 67.

[2] Children's Employment Commission (1862) : *Sixth Report, Parl. Pap.* 1867, XVI, p. xviii.

[3] Children's Employment Commission (1862) : *Sixth Report : Parl. Pap.* 1867, XVI, xxiv.

carried conviction, for on 2nd April, 1867, the House was induced to pass a resolution ' That in the opinion of this House, the employment of women and children in agriculture should be regulated, as far as may be, by the principles of the Factory Acts ', and to reappoint the Commissioners, H. S. Tremenheere and E. C. Tufnell, for a more extended inquiry into the subject.[1]

As regards the number of children affected, the problem was one of considerable importance. At the census of 1861 there were more than 40,000 children under twelve years of age employed in outdoor agricultural work.[2] Whilst conditions in respect of education varied to some extent in the various parts of the country, there was evidence that they were growing worse rather than better.[3] ' The maximum school age has been steadily and almost continuously lessening for the last 10 years,' wrote the assistant commissioner who visited Norfolk, Essex, Sussex, and Gloucestershire. ' In agricultural districts it has become a rare thing to find a labourer's son in the schools above the age of 10.'[4] ' Many [children] cease to obtain any effective instruction whatever after seven or eight

[1] *Hansard* 1867, CLXXXVI, p. 1025.

[2] Commission on the Employment of Children, etc., in Agriculture (1867) : *Second Report : Parl. Pap.* 1868-69, XIII, xx.

[3] The county of Northumberland and parts of the county of Durham were exceptional. Here the employment on farms of children under 10 was practically nowhere found, and it was the custom to keep the children at school up to 12 to 14 years of age. *Cf. Mr Henley's Report, passim :* Employment of Children in Agriculture Commission (1867) : *Parl. Pap.* 1867-68, XVII. Also : ' The general state of the wage-classes [in Northumberland] is so satisfactory, that I have no hesitation in asserting that if all England had been like it, this Commission ought not to have been issued.' *Mr Tuffnell's Report : Parl. Pap.* 1868-69, XIII, p. lxv.

[4] Employment of Children, etc., in Agriculture (1867) : *First Report : Parl. Pap.* 1867-68, XVII, *Appendix, Rev. J. Fraser's Report*, p. 18.

years of age, and in some parishes it is the maximum age to which they can be kept at school,' it was reported of Dorsetshire.[1] The cause was commonly to be found in the lowness of the wages of the agricultural labourers, which made the latter anxious to send their children out to work to augment the family income.

The two Commissioners, Tremenheere and Tuffnell, were not agreed as to the remedy. Tremenheere suggested as a solution (1) that every child employed in agriculture should be under the obligation to make 160 school attendances in each year until the age of twelve years ; (2) this obligation should be reduced to 60 attendances for any child of the age of nine and upwards who passed an examination in the fourth standard ; (3) it should cease altogether for any child who at the age of eleven or at any time between that age and the completion of its twelfth year can pass in the fifth standard.[2] That the 80 days of attendance required under (1) might be taken at irregular periods of the year, Tremenheere realised, but thought that ' the natural and imperious demand for children's labour in agriculture ', varying as it did as to season in different parts of the country, made this inevitable. By providing that the attendance at school might cease at the age of eleven, if the child passed the fifth standard, he hoped the employers would be induced to encourage more regular attendance and progress during the early years of the child's school life.[3] Tuffnell, on the other hand, was against making a certain amount of attendance at school

---

[1] Employment of Children, etc., in Agriculture (1867) : *Second Report* . *Parl. Pap.* 1868-69, XIII, *Appendix, Mr E. Stanhope's Report*, p. 6.

[2] The Employment of Children, etc., in Agriculture Commission (1867) ; *Second Report : Parl. Pap.* 1868-9, XIII, *Mr Tremenheere's Report*, p. xxii.

[3] *Ibid.*, xxiii.

compulsory as a condition of employment, and recommended that the employment of children in agricultural work should, except during the ten weeks of school holidays, be prohibited before the age of nine—hoping that after two years it would be possible to raise this age to ten, and then ultimately to eleven or twelve.[1]

Although these final Reports of the two Commissioners were not made until October 1869, and although a few years more were to elapse before any general legislative provision was to be made, the matter was not allowed to go without consideration by Parliament. In 1867 two Bills were introduced, one,[2] sponsored by Lord Shaftesbury, to deal with the problem of employment in ' agricultural gangs ', and the other,[3] introduced by Mr H. Fawcett and others, to provide for the better education of children employed in agriculture generally. In Fawcett's Bill the proposal was simply that every child of less than thirteen years of age employed in agriculture should be compelled to attend school on alternate days. Children living more than three miles from any school might be excused from attending ; and also the magistrates might suspend the operation of the Act for two months in each year at harvest time.[4] Lord Shaftesbury's Bill was on different lines. It provided that no child under eight should be employed in a ' gang '. It had been the intention also as regards education to follow the system of the Printworks Act and to require the children to attend school for 400 hours during the half year ending 31st March and for 200 hours

---

[1] *Ibid., Mr Tuffnell's Report*, pp. lx, lxxiii.
[2] *Parl. Pap.* 1867, I, p. 49.
[3] *Ibid.*, p. 45.
[4] *Hansard* 1867, CLXXXVII, p. 559.

during the other half.[1] The latter part of the proposals, however, appears to have been eliminated in the House of Lords, for the Bill as brought to the House of Commons contained no reference to schooling,[2] and in the form in which it was passed it did no more so far as children were concerned than prohibit the employment in an agricultural gang of children under the age of eight.[3]

It was then within two or three weeks of the end of the Parliamentary session, and as there was considerable opposition shown to the proposals of Mr Fawcett's measure it was inevitable that in the rush and pressure of business the Bill should fail to make any further progress.

In view of the activities during 1867 to 1869 of the Commission on the Employment of Children in Agriculture, the efforts of those who were seeking to improve the lot of the children employed in this way were relaxed for a time. On 25th June, 1869, Mr Fawcett called the attention of the House of Commons to the reports of and the evidence collected by the assistant commissioners, urging the importance of early legislation being passed. It was impossible, he said,[4] to impose legislative interference on any branch of industry without occasioning some temporary disturbance of it, and no scheme could be devised that would not involve some trouble to the farmer, and some apparent hardship to the labourer. But would not these inconveniences, he asked, be a hundred times compensated for by the advantages that would ensue ? He opposed Lord Shaftesbury's remedy of exacting a certain number

[1] *Hansard* 1867, CLXXXVIII, p. 1662.

[2] *Parl. Pap.* 1867, I, p. 49.

[3] *Cf. Hansard* 1867, CLXXXIX, pp. 487-518. 30 and 31 Vict., c. 130.

[4] *Hansard* 1869, CXCVII, pp. 582-592.

of hours of school attendance in a year, on the lines of the Printworks Act, and advocated the alternate day system. On this occasion most of the speakers were agreed that something would have to be done. Clearly, one member said, Parliament must interfere : 'Compulsion in some shape, such as was applied to the manufacturing districts, must be extended to the agricultural classes also.' But as to what form that compulsion was to be applied he should be cautious in expressing any decided opinion.[1] So, awaiting the final recommendations of the Commission, and in the absence of any strong body of opinion in favour of this system or that, the subject was once more shelved. Mr Fawcett continued to be the chief protagonist on the side of education, and on 27th May, 1870, he again introduced the question, this time more particularly with the final report of the Commission in view. Some of his arguments have a present-day ring about them. 'It was said that the farmer wanted the labour of the child ; but to that he replied that the evidence before the Commission brought out the fact that the prosperity of agriculture varied inversely with the age at which children were sent to work. In Northumberland, where children were rarely sent to work until they were 12 years old, a superior class of agricultural labourer was to be found ; and in consequence the farmers were able to pay 20, or 30, or even 40 per cent. more wages for labour than in the worst counties of England.' Mr Culley, who investigated for the Agricultural Commission, stated that so superior was the labourer in Northumberland in conse-quence of increased intelligence resulting from the practice of not sending the children to work until they were 12

[1] *Ibid.*, p. 602.

years old, that the labourer, on account of his increased
efficiency, was enabled to receive higher wages. Upon the
point whether it was necessary for a child to go to
work at eight or nine years of age in order to
learn his trade, added Mr Fawcett, the evidence
given before the Commission was conclusive. Mr Fraser
and other Commissioners had examined the labourers,
and their testimony was unanimously to the effect that it
was not necessary for a child to go to work at that early
age, and that a child would learn his trade better if kept
at school until he was 12 years old. The poverty of the
parents was urged as a most formidable objection to the
adoption of a system of compulsion in respect to the
schooling of the children, because the parents, it was said,
could not afford to lose any portion of the earnings of their
children. On the other hand, a good deal was to be said
in favour of a general system of compulsion, which would
limit the supply of juvenile labour throughout the country,
and thereby directly increase its price. At the same time,
it would indirectly produce important effects on the
wages of adult labour, for nothing more depressed the
wages of adult labour than the competition of juvenile
labour.[1] H. A. Bruce, the Home Secretary, urged in reply
that the matter should await the decision of the House in
regard to the compulsory provisions of the Education
Bill.[2] The latter would, if passed, authorize the appointment of local School Boards with power to make school
attendance compulsory within their districts. He wanted
to see the compulsory principle applied gradually rather
than generally and immediately.

A further attempt was made in 1872, when a Bill ' to

[1] *Hansard* 1870, CCI, pp. 1553-4.
[2] *Forster's Elementary Education Bill* 1870.

regulate the employment of children in agriculture in England and Wales '[1] was introduced by Mr Clare Read, Kay-Shuttleworth and others. It proposed first, to prohibit the employment of children under eight years in agricultural work ; secondly, that it should not be lawful ' to employ in any year any child above the age of eight years . . . unless the parent of such child has obtained a certificate to the effect that such child has completed, if under ten years of age, 250 school attendances, if above ten years, 150 school attendances, during the twelve months preceding the 31st December immediately preceding such year '. By this time, however, the Government were feeling their way towards a system of general compulsory education, as against extending the system of indirect compulsion of the Bill and of the Factory Acts. W. E. Forster said that the Government not only did not oppose the Bill but were obliged to the introducers for having taken the matter up. He went on to doubt whether the age should be limited to twelve years, and expressed the view that the numbers of school attendances proposed were surely too small, and that it might be necessary to make them more consecutive to obtain greater regularity.[2] Obviously, the way was clearing for some definite action ; and though the Bill had to be withdrawn at the end of the session of 1872, a similar Bill was brought forward at the beginning of the following year.[3] On this occasion the House of Commons went one step further than the promoters of the Bill and raised the upper age for school attendance from twelve

[1] *Parl. Pap.* 1872, I, p. 27.
[2] *Hansard* 1872, CCXI, p. 1660.
[3] *Parl. Pap.* 1873, I, p. 11.

N

to thirteen.[1] The House of Lords restored the original age in the Bill, however,[2] as well as provided for the exemption from the prescribed penalties of persons employing children in hay and corn harvesting and in hop gathering.[3] The main provisions of the Act, which came into effect on 1st January, 1875, were these[4] :—

(a) The employment in agricultural work of children under eight was prohibited ;

(b) Children above eight and under twelve could not be employed unless they were certified as having completed, if under ten, 250 school attendances and, if ten years and upwards, 150 school attendances within a period commencing not more than twelve months immediately before the month in which the certificate was issued. These attendances had to be notified in a certificate to be signed by the principal teacher of a school recognised by the Committee of the Privy Council on Education as giving efficient elementary education ; and the certificate was not valid for more than twelve months ;

(c) In the case of children who obtained from one of H.M. Inspectors of Schools a certificate of having reached the fourth standard the provisions of (b) did not apply ;

(d) The age prescribed in the Agricultural Gangs Act of 1867, under which children should not be employed in gangs, was raised from eight to ten.

Unfortunately no machinery was set up under the Act

[1] *Hansard* 1873, CCXV, p. 1458.
[2] *Hansard* 1873, CCXVI, p. 1153.
[3] *Cf. Lords Amendments : Parl. Pap.* 1873, I, p. 17.
[4] 36 and 37 Vict., c. 67.

to ensure that its provisions were carried out. On an inquiry being addressed in 1875 by the Home Office to the Chairmen of Quarter Sessions, it became clear that in many counties the Act was practically of no effect. From Berks it was reported that the Act ' is not working effectually because there is no machinery for enforcing its provisions ' ; from Essex, that it was ' practically inoperative . . . it is in their [the magistrates'] opinion essential that some public officers should be employed to enforce the Act ' ; from Lincolnshire, that 'there have been very few cases brought before the Justices for infringement of the Act : that there is but little doubt there are frequent violations of the provisions of the Act, but that there appears to be an indisposition on the part of individuals to take proceedings against delinquents ' ; from Warwick, that 'the provisions of the Act do not appear to be carried out . . . no case in any instance has been brought before the magistrates to enforce the Act '.[1] The Inspectors of Schools bore testimony to the same effect. ' I cannot say ', reported the Inspector for the county of Worcester, ' that the Agricultural Children's Act has had much effect as yet upon the parents and employers. The managers of schools have, in many instances, been most active in making known the provisions of the Bill, by posting up a copy of it in the schoolroom, by circulating leaflets containing it among their parishioners. . . . These well-intentioned warnings, however, have seldom met with any response or resulted in any marked increase in school attendance, but, on the contrary, have generally been treated with indifference . . . from an unwillingness to believe that the Act would

[1] *Correspondence Relative to the Operation of the Agricultural Children's Act : Parl. Pap.* 1875, LXI, pp. 4-15.

ever be enforced.'[1] In the following year the Inspector for the counties of Suffolk and Essex reported that ' to the great regret of those who desire the extension of elementary education among the labouring classes ', the Act was wholly inoperative[2]; and similar evidence was forthcoming from the Inspectors in other counties.[3]

This unsatisfactory state of affairs was terminated, however, by the repeal of the Agricultural Children's Act on the passing in 1876 of the Elementary Education Act, under which attendance at school became generally compulsory as from 1st January, 1877.[4]

[1] *Report of the Committee of Council on Education*, 1874-75 : *Parl. Pap.* 1875, XXIV, p. 314.

[2] *Report of the Committee of Council on Education*, 1875-76 : *Parl. Pap.* 1876, XXIII, p. 331.

[3] *Cf. Ibid.*, p. 338 (Devon) ; p. 385 (Gloucester and Somerset). Also *Parl. Pap.* 1877, XXIX, p. 465 (Berks).

[4] *Cf. infra.* p. 213.

CHAPTER VII

LEGISLATION FOR ALL INDUSTRIES

THE investigations of the Factories Inquiry Commission of 1833, though predominantly concerned with the textile industries, had in fact extended to other branches of industry. At this period, however, outside the textile factories, there was comparatively little industry carried on in factories.[1] In Birmingham, for example, the Commissioners of 1833 had found that there was practically ' no establishment where children were collected together in large numbers to work together, as is the case in cotton, woollen, and flax mills.' A pin factory and a button factory were the only exceptions.[2] At Wolverhampton, there were only two factories—one for japanning, the other a brass and screw factory—and at these but few children were employed.[3] The earthenware and porcelain industry

---

[1] Cf. ' The establishment of factory industry was a very much slower process than used to be supposed. The tendency of many historians to ante-date the general adoption of machinery is due to ascribing too much importance to the actual date of an invention. Early machinery was clumsy, costly, and greedy of fuel. Constant breakdowns caused endless trouble, and it was difficult to find skilled workers for repairs. Many employers were men of small means, and most of them were conservative minded. The scales were heavily weighted against machinery, and it is not surprising that in most industries its adoption was relatively slow.' Health, Wealth, and Population, 1760-1815. Buer, M. (1926), p. 57.

[2] Factory Inquiry Commission : First Report : Parl. Pap. 1833, XX, p. 900.

[3] Ibid., p. 1091.

of Staffordshire was one of the very few in which factories employing considerable numbers of children could be said to exist in 1833. For the children employed in the potteries, however, twelve and thirteen hours' work a day was the usual practice ; and seven and eight years was a common age for the children to begin work.[1]

It was not until the sub-commissioners of the Children's Employment Commission of 1841[2] had completed their investigations that a detailed account of the state of child employment in industry generally, other than in textile factories, was made available. By this time, the employment of children in factories had become much more general in the metal trades. In every one of the numerous workshops of Birmingham, for example, children were employed. Many—the youngest, on the whole—were 'pin-headers', and of six of these taken at random, the average age was rather less than eight. Though a good deal of the employment was not of a laborious kind, in some processes, such as piercing, press-work, and brass filing, it involved considerable physical strain, ' especially when, as so often happens, very young children six, seven, or eight years old are concerned '.[3] In Sheffield, 840 children under thirteen were employed in various branches of the metal trades—as knife-hafters, type-founders, silver-platers, nail and screw makers, and grinders. In hafting, which employed the bulk of these children, the latter started work as early as eight years of age. Grinding, on account of the inhalation of the dust of the stone and steel,

---

[1] *Ibid.*, pp. 1011-1060.

[2] *Cf. supra*, p. 108.

[3] Children's Employment Commission : *Appendix to the Second Report : Parl. Pap.* 1843, XIV, p. F19.

was described as 'perhaps the most pernicious of any branch of manufacture in England '.[1] The manufacture of glass gave employment to a considerable number of young children, especially in parts of Lancashire, in the Stourbridge district, and in London.[2] In the porcelain and earthenware trades of Staffordshire, there were 1500 children employed under thirteen years of age.[3] Much of this latter employment was very unhealthy, those employed as ' mould-runners ' being constantly at work in a temperature ranging from 100° to 130°.[4] Paper-making, rope and twine making, tobacco manufacture, printing and bookbinding, dressmaking and millinery, were examples of other industries in which the employment of young children was found. Some of the worst cases of the excessive employment of children were seen in occupations where they were employed singly or in very small numbers. In the case of brick-making, for example, a sub-commissioner found a boy of ten years of age, who carried bricks from 3 a.m. to 9 p.m., during which time he carried 7,000 bricks and travelled over a distance of 20 miles.[5]

Everywhere, it was found, the children in factory employment were unable to attend day schools, and were too much fatigued after their day's work to attend night schools. The number of schools available, moreover, was altogether inadequate. The population of Sheffield was estimated to be 123,000, of whom about one-fifth, or

[1] *Report of Sub-Commissioner* (J. C. Symons) : *Ibid.*, E1 and 2.
[2] Children's Employment Commission : *Second Report : Parl. Pap.* 1843, XIII, p. 20.
[3] *Ibid.*, p. 20.   [4] *Ibid.*, p. 45.
[5] Children's Employment Commission : *Appendix to Second Report : Parl. Pap.* 1843, XIV, B49.

24,600, were children between the ages of three and thirteen. Yet the day schools of every description, good and bad, comprised only 8,000 children, and the average daily attendance was fewer than 6,000.[1] With so early a leaving age as was necessitated by the low age at which the children were taken into employment, it is not surprising that the sub-commissioner for Sheffield reported that not a third of those who had been in employment could read and write with even moderate proficiency.

Parliament, however, appeared to be largely indifferent to the matter.[2] As has already been described, the textile industries, in which the conditions had been the most scandalous, were dealt with under the Factory Act of 1844, and the employment of children in calico print-works, under an Act passed in the following year. But there, except for the Act excluding children under ten years from mines, Parliamentary action ended ; and not until 1860 was a further extension beyond these industries seriously considered. In that year Parliament had under consideration the Mines Act.[3] On 26th April, 1860, a Bill,[4] designed to have a wide and general application to child employment, was introduced privately. The main clause of this Bill

[1] *Ibid.*, E20.

[2] ' It is a strange proof of the general neglect of the morals and health of the children of the working classes, that this Report [Children's Employment Commission, 1843] lay unnoticed for twenty years, during which the children thus " bred up without the remotest sign of comprehension as to what is meant by the term morals, who had neither knowledge, nor religion, nor natural affection," were allowed to become the parents of the present generation.' Nassau W. Senior, in *Transactions of the National Association for the Promotion of Social Science*, 1863, p. 63.

[3] *Cf. supra*, p. 157.

[4] *Bill to Provide for the Education of Children Employed in Manufactures or Other Regular Labour : Parl. Pap.* 1860, III, p. 139. Introduced by Mr Adderley.

provided that it should be unlawful to employ in whole-time work in any manufacturing process or in any regular work any child under the age of twelve years, unless the employer first obtained the certificate of a schoolmaster, showing that the child was able to read and write. This Bill was opposed on behalf of the Government by the Home Secretary, Sir George Lewis, in a speech which contained some points of interest. The Bill, he declared, had a close connection with the Mines Bill lately under consideration. The first instance of exceptional legislation of the kind had been in regard to the factory children.[1] That had been because it had been thought the children employed in factories were in a peculiar condition. Parliament had seen an existing evil, which could not be disputed, and had applied a remedy for it in the case of a certain limited class, without caring for any logical objections that might be made as to the inconsistency of legislating for one class alone. Then in the case of the children employed in mines, it had been thought desirable to introduce into the Mines Bill a clause providing that no child should be employed in any mine who could not read or write and that, when so employed, he should attend school. Mr Adderley, who had introduced the Bill then under discussion, had taken the view that all this was inconsistent, and that what applied to mines and factories should be extended to all classes of employment.[2] Now,

[1] The term ' factory children ', as used in these early discussions, meant children employed in the textile mills and factories.

[2] *Cf.* Paper by Rev J. P. Norris, H.M. Inspector of Schools, on *The Education Bill of Last Session* [viz., Adderley's Bill] : ' The mill-owner, the bleacher, and now the coal-master are trammelled by legislative restrictions, while all other employers of labour are free. The potter and the ironmaster may employ children at any age, for any number of hours in the day, while their neighbours—the spinners, and weavers, and bleachers,

he (Sir George Lewis) was not prepared to say that that argument might not gradually force its way into the minds of the community ; indeed he himself concurred in the justice of it in the abstract.   But in this country we did not in general make our laws according to the rules of the great logicians ; we did not act upon abstract principles, but took up particular cases as they occurred, and endeavoured to feel our way from one case to another. By this experimental method, he concluded, we were much more successful than if we pursued a more rapid and perhaps more logical course.[1]   Mr W. E. Gladstone, then Chancellor of the Exchequer, expressed with a gay contempt the Government's view of the futility of the measure. The passing of such a Bill, he said, was as much out of the question as a Bill to abolish the House of Commons.

and coal-masters can only employ them under certain educational restrictions.   Clearly, I think—so clearly that when stated it seems a truism— all or none ought to be restricted . . . What is the result ?—that the children are forsaking restricted employments, and flocking to those that are unrestricted.   The factory inspectors, while they unanimously commend the educational effect of the Factory Act, confess at the same time that there has been a serious diminution in the number of children employed in mills.   Since the passing of these Acts, numbers of children have left their half-time employment in the mill, to seek full-time employment at an earlier age elsewhere.   The same will be the case in our collieries.   The difficulty of finding an adequate supply of young hands is daily increasing, and will go on increasing if other employments continue to be unrestricted . . . We must recede or advance in this course of legislation.   To recede —to go back to the frightful evils of the old factory and colliery system, described in the Reports of the Children's Employment Commissioners, but now happily a matter of bygone history, would be an infatuation. Advance we must ; political economy and education alike demand it. The Economist demands that all or none should be restricted, and the Educationalist demands that the undoubted blessings of the factory legislation should be extended to other classes of children.'   *Transactions of the National Association for the Promotion of Social Science*, 1860, p. 389.

[1] *Hansard* 1860, CLIX, pp. 2022, 2023.

Relegate the subject to debating societies, for which it might be an excellent theme : it was the habit of the House to proceed with reference to practical duties.[1]   In the face of this attitude, it was inevitable that the Bill (which indeed had not been drawn up with sufficient skill, or, apparently, with sufficient knowledge of the difficulties to be provided against) should make no progress.

In the following year, 1861, Lord Shaftesbury[2] secured the appointment of another Commission to inquire into the employment of children and young persons in trades not already affected by legislation.   In raising the question in the House of Lords, he said that since the Report of the Children's Employment Commission in 1842, the evils therein described had in some instances been mitigated, and in others had been aggravated and increased.   More-over, some old trades had become extinct, and, on the other hand, some new trades had been started.[3]   It was clearly desirable, therefore, that a fresh inquiry should be held. The Commissioners appointed for the purpose in February 1862 were H. S. Tremenheere, R. D. Grainger, and E. C. Tuffnell ; and, as in the case of several previous Com-missions of a similar kind, assistant commissioners were appointed to assist, primarily by making detailed investi-gations in particular districts.[4]   Inquiry was first directed to certain trades in which either the employers or the workpeople, or both, had shown a disposition in favour of

---

[1] *Hansard* 1860, CLIX, p. 2025.

[2] Lord Ashley had succeeded to the title in 1851.

[3] *Hansard* 1861, CLXIV, 1875-1879.

[4] The Assistant Commissioners were Francis Davy Longe, B.A., of Oriel College, Oxford, barrister-at-law ; John Edward White, M.A., Fellow of New College, Oxford, barrister-at-law ; Henry Wm. Lord, M.A., late Fellow of Trinity College, Cambridge, barrister-at-law,

legislation being applied to them, and to others, coming within the category of ' noxious trades ', which were well known to be causing serious injury to the health of those engaged in them. The Commission's First Report,[1] made in June 1863, dealt chiefly with the following trades: pottery, lucifer matches, percussion caps, paper staining, and fustian cutting.

In the pottery manufacture,[2] it was ascertained, some 4,500 children under thirteen years of age were employed. ' Turning the jigger ' and ' mould running ' (carrying the ware on the moulds into the heated stove-rooms, and the moulds back again to the man making the articles) formed the chief employments ; and both, carried on as they were during a long day, were very hard work for boys, most of whom began at a very young age—six, seven, and eight years being not unusual. Exposed to such hard labour, to highly heated rooms, and to an atmosphere of fine dust, it was inevitable that the constitutions of these children were seriously injured and that pulmonary diseases were very prevalent. As for the educational state of the children, whereas in the country districts of the county, 43 per cent. of the children left school before reaching the age of ten, in the potteries the proportion was 75 per cent. and was increasing. Of the 256 children in one of the Sunday schools in a pottery town, most of whom were mould-runners and jigger turners, 138 could not read the Testament, and 127 could not write their names.[3] The

---

[1] Children's Employment Commission (1862) : *First Report : Parl. Pap.* 1863, XVIII.

[2] Some of the leading employers in the Staffordshire potteries had themselves recently petitioned Parliament to deal with the employment of children. *Ibid.*, p. 322.

[3] Evidence of Rev H. Sandford, Inspector of Schools, *Ibid.*, p. 120.

need, therefore, observed the Commissioners, of introducing the half-time system for this mass of children ' among whom elementary instruction is so partially diffused ' was apparent. The recommendation of the Commissioners was accordingly to the effect that the provisions of the Factory Act should be extended to the potteries ; and further, that a certificate of a certain minimum amount of education should be required as a condition of employment.[1]

The lucifer match trade was a comparatively new one. It dated only from the year 1833, when the discovery of means of applying phosphorus to the match itself had been made. By 1845 the existence of the painful and loathsome disease known as ' phosphorus disease ' or ' phossy jaw ' had been noted. At the time of the Commission's inquiry, the number of children and young persons employed in this way was about 1,800, many of the children being employed in the processes of ' mixing ', ' dipping ', ' drying ', etc., in which the largest amount of vapour was given off by the phosphorus and inhaled by the children, leading in the long run to disease. Some of the largest factories had adopted regulations (e.g. the non-employment of children with decayed teeth) to minimise this evil, but there was clearly an urgent need to enforce adequate sanitary precautions on all. Specific recommendations to this effect were accordingly made by the Commissioners, who recommended also that no child should be employed in the processes referred to otherwise than on alternate days, or for other hours than those permitted by the Factory Act. ' It may be expected ', remarked the Commissioners, ' that the increased intelligence arising

[1] Children's Employment Commission (1862) : *First Report : Parl. Pap.* 1863, XVIII, p. 46.

from extended education under the half-time system of the Factory Act, will lead the young to know the value and importance of carefully availing themselves of these means [of cleanliness], and thus doing their part to secure for themselves an exemption from the disorders which now affect so large a number of them in this occupation.'[1] Employment in percussion cap factories was another dangerous occupation, and several explosions had recently occurred resulting in the loss of lives and serious injuries to others, of whom many were young girls. To this trade also, then, it was recommended that the entire provisions of the Factory Acts should extend.[2]

The making of paper hangings, or paper staining—the printing of a pattern in colours on sheets of paper—provided employment for about 650 children under 13 years of age ; and though the work in itself was not too laborious, the hours of work were inordinately long, 6 a.m. to 9 p.m. being usual for the greater part of the year. As regards the education of the children, the sub-commissioner who investigated this trade reported : ' In the course of visiting the various works . . . I have made it a practice to test to some degree the extent of education among the children and young persons. I have endeavoured to do this by requiring some of ten years of age and upwards, whom I picked out as they worked, and who appeared to be fair average instances of their class, to read a few lines of a simple hymn from a small book printed in a type rather superior to that of the ordinary hymn book. The majority have at once admitted that they could not read

[1] Children's Employment Commission (1862) : *First Report : Parl. Pap.* 1863, XVIII, pp. 48-56.
[2] *Ibid.*, p. 58.

at all ; and, as it did not appear to me that those, who thought they could, were generally disposed to shrink from being tested, I have confined any further investigation to the minority, of whom very few could read with ease. Most spelt the words letter by letter, some did not know all their letters ; in most cases when the reading was at all good home teaching rather than school seems to have produced that result, except in instances of children who had been for perhaps a year or more consecutively employed as " half timers " in a factory. In the north, speaking generally, the great majority of those children, whom I found capable of reading and of understanding what they read, had been for some lengthened period in a factory school.'[1]

Fustian cutting provided occupation for over 500 children under thirteen years of age, most of whom began at nine or ten, though cases of employment as young as seven were found. Fourteen hours a day (including meal times) was the average working time of a child—though employment was apt to be irregular. Not only were the hours long but the work was often heavy and unhealthy, with the result that deformities of the knee, ankle, shoulder, or spine, as well as stunted growth were common. Because of the physical disabilities to which the employment of children as fustian cutters gave rise, the Commissioners recommended that while the provisions of the Factory Acts should apply to this occupation, they should be modified so as to prohibit the employment of children before the age of eleven years.[2]

---

[1] Children's Employment Commission (1862) : *First Report : Parl. Pap.* 1863, XVIII, pp. 217-218.

[2] *Ibid.*, p. 79.

In the following year (1864) the Government brought in a Bill[1] to give effect to these recommendations. Little opposition to it was manifested. The suitability of the Factory Acts had by now become well established and generally accepted. In putting forward the Bill on behalf of the Government, Mr H. A. Bruce said that there was not one member who had opposed the introduction of the early Factory Acts who did not now admit that he had been wrong ; these Acts so far from having proved an evil had been a great blessing. Yet the Government did not intend to interfere in any industry without sufficient reason being shown. Fortunately, the report of the Commissioners spared the necessity of using much argument in the case of the new Bill.[2]

This Factory Acts Extension Act 1864[3] extended the provisions of the Factory Acts (ensuring the half-time attendance at school of children concerned) to children employed in the manufacture of earthenware, lucifer matches, percussion caps, cartridges, and to those employed in paper staining and in fustian cutting. Its application was to be gradual : for periods of six months and two and a half years children not less than eleven and twelve years respectively might be employed as ' young persons '. In the case of fustian cutting, the employment of children under the age of eleven was forbidden. The total number of children engaged in all these occupations, however, was comparatively small, probably fewer than 7,000.[4]

[1] *A Bill for the Extension of the Factory Acts : Parl. Pap.* 1864, II, p. 81.

[2] *Hansard* 1864, CLXXV, p. 1710.

[3] 27 and 28 Vict., c. 48.

[4] According to H. S. Tremenheere, this Act affected about 50,000 all told, ' of whom probably about 30,000 were children, young persons and women '. *Transactions of the National Association for the Promotion of Social Science,* 1865, p. 301.

During the next three years the investigations of the Commissioners embraced a great variety of trades and manufactures, in respect of which several reports were issued. In the lace trade, the majority of the processes, e.g. ' finishing ' and ' dressing ', remained outside the scope of the Act of 1861.[1] The latter had applied to lace making only, in which about 10,000 out of the total of 150,000 persons employed in the trade were concerned.[2] Many of these children, moreover, were employed in private houses (in ' drawing, mending, and joining the pieces of net which had recently been taken from the machine'), often under worse conditions and at earlier ages than those obtaining in the factories and warehouses. The manufacture of hosiery, which at the time of the Children's Employment Commission of 1841-2 had been almost entirely a handwork industry, had since become mainly a machine industry, though much of it had continued to be carried on in private houses. In the ' warehouses ', in which the bulk of the children were employed, the hours of work were shorter than in factories ; ten or eleven hours a day was usual, and twelve hours and more not uncommon.[3] Many children were engaged in connection with the working of ' hand frames ', either in ' shops, or as they are sometimes called, small factories, consisting of one or more rooms, and containing from 10 to 20, 30, 40 or even nearly double that number of frames, owned and superintended by masters ', or in cottages and small rooms in private houses containing a few frames, worked by a man and his

[1] *Cf. supra*, p. 135.
[2] Children's Employment Commission (1862) : *Second Report : Parl. Pap.* 1864, XXII, p. 5.
[3] *Ibid.*, pp. 32-33.

O

family.[1] Lighting and ventilation were generally deficient, and the hours of work irregular and excessive. The age at which the children (of whom, out of the 120,000 persons engaged in the hosiery trade, there were several thousands) began work varied, from ten to twelve being usual for work at ' frames ', while boys often began as ' winders ' at six, seven, or eight.[2] Some 6,000 children were engaged in the manufacture of straw plait, chiefly in the counties of Hertford, Buckingham and Bedford. Plaiting was taught in ' schools ', to which the children were commonly put at the age of four. Up to the age of seven the children remained in the ' school ' from 9 a.m. to 1 p.m. and from 2 p.m. to 4 p.m. ; but from seven onwards up to the age of twelve or fourteen they returned in the evening from 5 p.m. to 8 p.m. There was rarely any attempt at education. The school proper was spoken of by the children as ' the reading school ' in contradistinction to the plait school, whose function was simply to keep the children at work and to see that they got through the task required of them by their parents. That it was testified by reliable witnesses that these children grew up in a state of lamentable ignorance is not surprising.[3] The making of wearing apparel—dressmaking, millinery, tailoring, glove-making, shoemaking and so on — accounted for a considerable number of children. Whereas at the Girls' National Schools in Yeovil (a town where gloving was a principal occupation) there were 150 children under seven in attendance, there were only 34 between seven and eight, and twelve over ten years of age. ' The result is that the children being

---

[1] *Ibid.*, p. 35.   [2] *Ibid.*, pp. 35, 36.
[3] *Ibid.*, p. 40.

taken away at so early an age, and no provision like that of half-time being made, they grow up utterly uneducated, and often unable to read.'[1]

The Third Report of the Commissioners dealt with employment in blast furnaces, rolling mills and furnaces, and miscellaneous metal manufactures,[2] as to which they recommended the abolition of night work for the young and the securing of the half-time system of hours of work and education for all under thirteen. The state of child employment in the Sheffield metal trades, of which an alarming account had been made more than twenty years previously by the Children's Employment Commission of 1841, was revealed as one most urgently in need of regulation. Children, beginning employment as young as ten years, and even earlier, were still employed in the deadly occupation of grinding, where the liability to inhale an atmosphere charged with dust inevitably led to ill health, and often to early death. Provision for enforcing better ventilation, as well as for restricting the incredibly long hours of work and the age at which boys might begin employment, was clearly an urgent need.[3] In South Staffordshire, 1,200 boys from eight to thirteen years of age were employed in the blast furnaces and in the mills and forges, many working night shifts from 6 p.m. to 6 a.m.[4] In Birmingham alone, 2,000 children under the age of *ten*

---

[1] *Ibid.*, p. 74.

[2] Children's Employment Commission (1862): *Third Report: Parl. Pap.* 1864, XXIX, p. 319.

[3] Children's Employment Commission (1862): *Fourth Report: Parl. Pap.* 1865, XX, pp. 108, 112.

[4] Children's Employment Commission (1862): *Third Report: Parl. Pap.* 1864, XXII, p. 324.

were employed in the ' general hardware and other manufactures ' ;[1] and between the ages of ten and thirteen
there were undoubtedly some thousands more. As for the
education of these children, the sub-commissioner gave an
analysis of an examination, as regards ' reading, spelling,
or telling letters,' of 80 children between the ages of seven
and sixteen at one large factory in Birmingham :

' Of these 72.5 per cent admitted that they could not
read, 13.75 practically could not, 12.5 could read a little,
and the remaining 1.25, i.e. one girl, could not read
effectually . . . Scattered through the evidence will be
found numbers who did not know the letters, though in
capitals, some not even great A, or could not read single
figures, or do the simplest counting, e.g. " 17 times 17 ",
" 9 and 17 ", " 17 from 30 " . . . As those whose
answers are given in detail were taken in most cases
without any selection from appearance, etc., and as a
rule are given equally, whether they showed knowledge
or ignorance, it may be assumed that the answers fairly
represent the general mental condition of the mass . . .
The book used for testing the power of reading, etc., was
a child's book pictured, with clearly printed hymns and
songs, consisting of simple words chiefly of one syllable.
In this, many who at first said they could read, quite
broke down, some knowing little more than the letters.'[2]

The investigations of the Commissioners, extending over
a period of four years, had now covered practically all forms
of industrial employment other than those already dealt
with by legislation, and agriculture. At the end of their
labours they summed their conclusion and hopes thus :

' We heartily trust that we may have thus in some

[1] *Ibid.*, p. 328.   [2] *Ibid.*, p. 409.

degree contributed to bring the time nearer when so many thousands of your Majesty's poorer subjects of the working classes—especially the very young and those of the tenderer sex—will be relieved from the totally unnecessary burden and oppression of night work ; will be confined to the reasonable hours and natural limits of the factory hours, with the established periods for meals and for rest and recreation ; will perform their daily labour under more favourable conditions, breathing purer air, amid greater cleanliness, and protected against causes especially injurious to health, and tending to depress their vigour and shorten their lives ; and finally, will be under the obligation, between the ages of eight and thirteen, of combining a certain and very useful amount of school instruction with wages-yielding employment, and thus benefiting themselves, and their country, by reaching, as may be hoped, when they grow up, a higher standard of morals and intelligence '.

On Parliament reassembling early in 1867, it was at once intimated, in the Queen's Speech, that Bills for the ' extension of the beneficial provisions of the Factory Acts to other trades specially reported on by the Royal Commission, and for the better regulation, according to the principle of those Acts, of workshops where women and children are largely employed ' would be introduced.[1] Accordingly on 1st March, 1867, Spencer Walpole, who had become the Home Secretary on the Tories coming into power, introduced two Bills,[2] one to apply to factories,

[1] *Hansard* 1867, CLXXXV, p. 6.
[2] *A Bill for the Extension of the Factory Acts : Parl. Pap.* 1867, III, p. 1. *A Bill for regulating the hours of labour for children, young persons, and women employed in workshops : Ibid.*, p. 133.

and the other to workshops, the dividing line between the two categories being establishments employing 100 persons. It was no longer necessary to justify *ab initio* State action in this matter : the principle had long been accepted in the series of Acts already described. As for interfering with parental rights, Spencer Walpole declared that there was a parental duty as well as a parental right. A parent's first duty was to see that his child was physically, mentally, and morally educated, in order to fulfil the various duties of life ; and if that duty be neglected, then the State, the parent of the country, must fill the place of the natural protector of the child.[1] Although there were still a few members who opposed legislation of this kind (one, for instance, proposed that the glass trade should be excluded on the grounds that ' the necessary skill could only be acquired by practice from a very early age '),[2] it was clear that, in general, all parties realized the urgency of the need for legislation ; and apart from reducing from 100 to 50 the number of employees above which an establishment should be regarded as a ' factory ' and below which as a ' workshop ', no amendments of importance were made, and the Bills were passed by the end of the session in August.

The Factory Acts Extension Act 1867[3] applied the provisions of the existing Factory Acts to factories of the following descriptions : blast furnaces, foundries, mills and forges ; the manufacture of machinery and of any article of metal, of india-rubber or gutta-percha, of paper, glass, and tobacco ; letterpress printing and bookbinding ;

[1] *Hansard* 1867, CLXXXV, pp. 1271-1279.
[2] *Hansard* 1867, CLXXXVI, p. 452.
[3] 30 and 31 Vict., c. 103.

and any premises in which 50 or more persons were employed in any manufacturing process—excluding textile factories, mines, and other industries which had already been legislated for separately. Sunday employment was prohibited, and the employment of children under twelve years in melting or annealing glass and of children under eleven years in grinding in the metal trades was made illegal. For a period of six months after 1st January, 1868, on which date the Act became operative, children not less than eleven years of age might be employed as if they were ' young persons ' ; and for a period of two and a half years, those not less than twelve years might be similarly employed ; and thus the introduction of the new regulations was, in accordance with previous practice, made gradual. For the children concerned, therefore, half-time attendance at school between the ages of eight and thirteen years was henceforward compulsory.

The Workshops Regulation Act 1867[1] provided that in establishments employing fewer than 50 persons in ' manual labour exercised by way of trade or for purposes of gain in or incidental to the making of any article ', no child should be employed (1) under the age of eight years ; (2) on any one day for more than six and a half hours (restricted to hours between 6 a.m. and 8 p.m.), or on Saturday afternoon or on Sunday ; (3) under the age of eleven in metal grinding or in fustian cutting. Every child should attend school for at least ten hours in every week. The provisions for weekly certificates of school attendance being obtained by the employer, for the deduction by the employer of a sum not exceeding 2d. per week from the child's wages for payment to the head

[1] 30 and 31 Vict., c. 146,

teacher of the school, and for empowering the Inspector of Factories to disqualify a teacher for granting certificates, followed those of the Factory Acts. While, however, under the Factory Acts Extension Act the responsibility for inspecting factories to ensure the enforcement of the statute was assigned to the Inspectors of Factories, under the Workshops Act the duty of inspection was assigned to the Local Authority.[1] In the case of this Act also, temporary provisions were made in order that the Act might come into effect gradually.

These two Acts affected a large proportion of the woman and child population of the country. The total number of women and children employed in the trades concerned had been stated to be 1,400,000,[2] of whom, of course, only a small proportion were children.

The question of extending the provisions of the Factory Acts to bleaching and dyeing works and to calico print-works, employment in which had been the subject of earlier legislation (Calico Printworks Act 1845, and the Bleaching and Dyeworks Act 1860) had been raised during the discussions of 1867. The Factory Inspectors also had continued to draw attention to the shortcomings of these two Acts.[3] Parliament decided, however, that before considering the matter a thorough inquiry should first be made into the operation of the two Acts concerned. This task was assigned to H. S. Tremenheere and E. C. Tuffnell, who had been responsible for the work of the Children's Employment Commission,[4] the detailed work of investi-

---

[1] This was terminated by an Act passed in 1871, workshops thereafter being inspected and reported on by the Inspectors of Factories.

[2] *Hansard* 1867, CLXXXV, p. 1273.

[3] *Reports of Inspectors of Factories : Parl. Pap.* 1864, XXII, p. 762.

[4] The third member of the Commission, R. D. Grainger, had recently died.

gation being undertaken by J. E. White who had carried out similar work for the Commissioners during the preceding years. The report was completed early in 1869.[1]

Under the Printworks Act children were liable to be employed between the hours of 6 a.m. and 10 p.m. and no Saturday half-holiday was provided for. The provision for education, which had long since been realised to be of very little value, was confined to requiring attendance at school for 150 hours every six months.[2] White made a careful and detailed investigation throughout the print-works district, visiting many works, interviewing employers and their managers, workers, and the like. The number of children so employed was estimated to be upwards of 4,000 in England and Scotland, the majority being in the Lancashire district.[3] The conclusion reached was, broadly, that there was no real reason why the Printworks Act should not be assimilated to the Factory Acts. The main diffi-culty would be to obtain a sufficient supply of children to meet the needs of the half-time system, but that difficulty was not peculiar to printworks and had been found susceptible to solution in the various other trades to which it applied.[4] The difficulties which had been found in the case of bleaching and dyeing works concerned the regu-lations applying to young persons and women, and need not here be dealt with.

The following year, 1870, an Act[5] was accordingly passed extending as from 1st January, 1872, the provisions of the

---

[1] *Report on the Printworks Act and on the Bleaching and Dyeing Works Acts : Parl. Pap.* 1868-9, XIV, p. 777.

[2] *Cf. supra*, p. 117.

[3] *Report on the Printworks Act, etc. : Mr J. E. White's Report : Parl. Pap.* 1868-9, XIV, p. 789.

[4] *Ibid.*, p. 798.   [5] 33 and 34 Vict., c. 62.

Factory Acts to printworks and to bleaching and dyeing works, and covering moreover a wider range of processes than had been affected by the two Acts previously applying to these trades.

The Factory Inspectorate had naturally had to be considerably enlarged to cope with the new duties devolving upon them, and had also been reorganised into two main districts, of which Alexander Redgrave and Robert Baker were respectively the principal Inspectors.[1] By 1868, Redgrave reported that he had now more than 15,000 works under his inspection, half of these being accounted for by the Factory Act of 1867.[2] The inspection of more than 5,000 works was similarly added by this Act in the district for which Baker was responsible.[3]

The reports of the Inspectors soon showed that the immediate effect of the new legislation was mainly to lead to the discharge of the children from employment, at least those under eleven, to whom the half-time provisions at once applied. In north Staffordshire the sub-inspector found that ' the direct educational effect of the law has been very small . . . there has certainly not been more than 25 children attending school under its provisions.'[4] In the Liverpool district, wrote the sub-inspector, ' I find almost everywhere that the restriction placed on the labour of children by the Factory Act Extension Act 1867 has quite put a stop to their employment. The occupiers of factories brought under by this Act will not go to the trouble of looking after their school attendance ; and the parents say that they can earn so little money as half-

[1] *Cf. Reports of Factory Inspectors : Parl. Pap.* 1875, XVI, pp. 72-73.
[2] *Reports of Inspectors of Factories : Parl. Pap.* 1868-69, XIV, p. 84.
[3] *Ibid.*, p. 211.   [4] *Ibid.*, p. 367.

timers that on their parts they would rather keep them at home and have no bother with the schooling.'[1] As regards the Birmingham district, too, it was reported that the half-time system had so far been a failure.[2] Manufacturers, stated Redgrave, would not, in the new circumstances, employ children unless they were essential to the manufacture or unless they were the cheapest labour that could be obtained. In the whole of his district, he reported in 1869, there were only 733 half-timers attending school under the Factory Act of 1867.[3]

This was clearly a state of affairs which had not been intended by Parliament. It was in marked contrast to the position in the textile trades, in which child employment had been subject to legislative control since 1833. In those trades the number of half-timers was increasing, and in 1868 amounted to a total of about 80,000.[4]

' I consider the time has arrived ', wrote Redgrave in 1869, ' when two material alterations may be made in the existing conditions. . . . First, that the age at which young persons may be employed for full time be raised by one year, i.e that children should work half-time and attend school until they are fourteen years of age instead of thirteen as at present. Second, that no young persons under the age of sixteen should be employed full-time unless a certificate be produced, given upon a prescribed form . . certifying that the young person can read and write well and work sums in the four first rules of simple

[1] *Ibid.*, p. 379.   [2] *Ibid.*, p. 389.   [3] *Ibid.*, p. 498.
[4] *Ibid.*, p. 479. *Cf. supra*, p. 82. The increase continued at a rapid rate, and in 1875 the number in the United Kingdom was 125,886. *Report of Factory and Workshops Act Commission, Appendix B : Parl. Pap.* 1876, XXIX.

arithmetic.'[1]   And the following year he went still further, advocating ' as an adjunct to the half-time system, the necessity of school attendance previous to employment being made a condition of employment.'[2]

In 1873, a Bill[3] was introduced by private Members, the chief of whom was Mundella, to secure further reform along the lines advocated by the Inspectors. Among its proposals were, (1) to raise the minimum age of employment to ten years, (2) to limit the daily period of work to five and a half hours, (3) to require in the case of a ' young person ' under fourteen years of age a certificate by an Inspector of Schools of having reached the ' third stardard ', before it should be legal to employ him otherwise than as a ' child ', and (4) to bring the silk manufacturing processes[4] under the same restrictions as other textile trades.   The Bill attempted, however, to restrict still further than had been the case hitherto the conditions of employment of women also, and it therefore encountered considerable opposition in this respect—though there was general sympathy for the proposals regarding children.   The Government promised to introduce in the following year a Bill on similar lines so far as children were concerned : the State was bound, said Assheton Cross, the Home Secretary, to interfere for the protection of the children ' to see that they were not overworked and that they were educated according to their station in life '.[5]   In introducing the Government Bill in 1874 Cross again laid emphasis on the necessity of children being educated, ' so that the country would get the benefit

---

[1] *Report of Inspectors of Factories : Parl. Pap.* 1868-9, XIV, p. 501.

[2] *Report of Inspectors of Factories : Parl. Pap.* 1870, XV, p. 115.

[3] *A Bill to Amend the Factory Acts : Parl. Pap.* 1873, I, p. 557.

[4] *Cf. supra*, p. 79.

[5] *Hansard* 1874, CCXVIII. p. 1793.

of having educated citizens when they grew up '. Little opposition was shown to the Bill, which passed through its various stages almost unaltered.[1] Unfortunately, its provisions were limited to the textile factories coming under the Factory Acts of 1833 and 1844, and those under the Lace Factory Act 1861, and did not extend to the larger number of factories and workshops embraced by the Acts of 1864 and 1867. The chief provisions of this Act were as follows :

(1) The age of employment was raised to ten years (nine years during the year 1875) ;

(2) After 1st January, 1876, a person of thirteen years and under fourteen should not be deemed a ' young person ' unless he had obtained a certificate of having attained a prescribed standard of proficiency in reading, writing and arithmetic ;[2]

(3) The hours of employment of a child should be limited to the hours either between 6 a.m. and 6 p.m. or between 7 a.m and 7 p.m. ;

(4) A child should not be employed continuously for more than four and a half hours without an interval of at least half an hour ;

---

[1] 37 and 38 Vict., c. 44.

[2] The standard prescribed was that for the ' Fourth Standard ', viz., ' Reading—To read with intelligence a few lines of poetry selected by the Inspector, and to recite from memory fifty lines of poetry.

Writing—Eight lines slowly dictated once from a reading book. Copy books to be shown. (Improved small hand).

Arithmetic—Compound rules, common weights and measures. (Note —The weights and measures taught in public elementary schools should be only such as are really useful, such as avoirdupois weight, long measure, liquid measure, time table, square and cubical measure, and any measure which is connected with the industrial occupations of the district.) ' *Reports of Factory Inspectors : Parl. Pap.* 1876, XVI, p. 79.

(5) Attendance at a school in England which was not recognised by the Education Department as giving efficient elementary instruction should not be deemed to be attendance at school for the purpose of the Acts ;

(6) The processes of silk manufacture should be brought, gradually, under the provisions of the Act.[1]

The limited application of this Act soon gave rise to a movement to secure an extension to trades other than those of the textile industry. The operation of the Workshops Act of 1867, also, had disclosed several serious weaknesses in its provisions. Up to 1872, during which time its enforcement had rested with the Local Authority, it had probably had little effect. Redgrave found, on taking over at the beginning of 1872 the duty of the inspection of workshops, that in the counties of Northampton, Bedford, Hertford and Bucks, which contained a very large number of workshops, there were only 120 half-timers attending school, which number, however, as a result of vigilant inspection, had increased to 1630 by the end of that year.[2] Moreover, the attendance at school up to a maximum of ten hours per week, required by the Workshops Act, could

---

[1] The number of children employed in the ' throwing and winding of raw silk ' had been as follows :

	1850	1856	1860	1867
11–13	4,581	5,042	5,182	4,121
u/11	1,423	1,550	1,832	764

' It is clear from the above that there is no care on the part of the silk throwsters to promote the education of the children they employ . . . That concession [viz., to employ children of 11 and over as " young persons ", vide the Factory Act 1844] has been the means, during the last 25 years, of depriving thousands of children of the education which, had they been in cotton factories, they must have enjoyed '. Redgrave, Reports of Inspectors of Factories : Parl. Pap. 1870, XV, p. 104.

[2] Reports of Inspectors of Factories : Parl. Pap. 1873, XIX, p. 61.

be made up in an irregular fashion. ' Managers and school-masters of inspected schools are ever ready to help, but when these little outcasts go to school when it pleases them, morning or afternoon, Monday, Tuesday or Wednesday, as caprice may dictate, disarranging organization, rendering teaching of little use, and in reality exercising a depressing influence on the school, when it is tested by a comparison of attendances with names on the books ; no one can be surprised that workshops children are not sought for or even considered desirable to be retained. Thus, after having induced managers to receive these half-time children, the results are generally so unsatisfactory that they are refused, generally upon the ostensible grounds that the school is overcrowded, and we are driven to accept mere apologies for schools, and, greatly to our dissatisfaction, to countenance what is after all a mere mockery of education.'[1] Assheton Cross indeed, on the matter being raised in Parliament in 1875, admitted that with different rules prevailing in different trades, the position was a confused one and could not be defended. He declared his determination to ensure that all children employed in manufactures should, as soon as possible, have the benefit of as much education and enjoy such advantages for health as legislation could secure for them.[2] At his suggestion, accordingly, a Royal Commission was appointed[3] charged with the duty of providing full in-formation on which further legislation could be based. Their work was pursued assiduously throughout the year

[1] Redgrave, *Reports of Inspector of Factories : Parl. Pap.* 1874, XIII, p. 197.   [2] *Hansard* 1875, CCXXII, p. 563.

[3] Sir James Fergusson, Lord Frederick Charles Cavendish, Lord Balfour of Burleigh, Sir Charles Du Cane, H. R. Brand, I. Knowles, and the O'Conor Don.

1875, examining the Inspectors of Factories, officials of the Factory and Education Departments, representatives of trade and manufactures, considering reports and returns, and visiting several districts to make a first-hand investigation. Their report[1] was submitted early in 1876. The Commissioners had, they stated in their *Report*, inquired, among other things, into the need for making legislative provision for the attendance of children at school, a ' subject now constantly from day to day receiving new illustration '.[2] They recommended that the Workshops Act should be repealed : ' there is no reason whatever why the regulations for securing such matters as the education of a child, the protection of life and limb . . . should be deliberately made less efficient in the smaller places of work, where they are likely to be more needed, in proportion to the greater facilities for escaping observation, than in the larger '.[3] In the field of education, the *Report* stated, it was impossible not to see that the result obtained fell far

[1] Factory and Workshops Acts Commission : *Report, with Minutes of Evidence, etc. :* Parl. Pap. 1876, XXIX and XXX.

[2] Factory and Workshops Acts Commission : *Report :* Parl. Pap. 1876, XXIX, x.

[3] Factory and Workshops Acts Commission : *Report :* Parl. Pap. 1876, XXIX, xvi. *Cf.* also the view of one of H.M. Inspectors of Schools : ' At present [1874] there exist many inefficient private adventure schools, attendances at which factory inspectors are obliged to accept, without question, as satisfying the Half-time Acts. It need hardly be remarked that there are many unworthy reasons which induce self-indulgent parents to prefer these schools to schools of recognized efficiency. The law itself is, moreover, much to blame in permitting *ten hours* school attendance to be accepted in lieu of five school attendances. I am happy to say that I have succeeded in inducing many managers to make a firm stand against the breach of discipline involved in yielding to employers in this matter. Were it possible rigidly to enforce the Workshops Act in my district [Leicester], the number of children regularly attending school would be largely increased. Both in towns and villages children are employed

short of what had been intended by the framers of the existing law, or that the law itself did not envisage all that it was possible and desirable to effect. The half-time system of school attendance, grounded upon indirect compulsion, had produced results considerable in themselves, more especially by reason of the regularity of attendance in places where the system had been fairly enforced. The attendance at school of a child for 13 or 14 hours a week all the year round, as a condition of his employment, which his parents cared more for than for his schooling, and an Inspector watching to see that it was carried out, often amounted to more hours of actual attendance than in the case of a child nominally attending whole time but with indifferent regularity. But now that compulsory whole time attendance was in many districts being enforced,[1] it was to be expected that half-timers, as compared with children under the jurisdiction of school boards using their compulsory powers, would fall more and more behind. Also, it was not enough to secure efficient education for the half-timers after they began to attend school ; it was essential to provide securely for their regular attendance before they went to work. Only so could they pursue their education with good effect and attempt to keep pace with the regular scholars. ' The schoolmaster who is charged with the task of getting the

chiefly at elastic webbing, and it is believed by those who have the means of knowing, that the law is habitually broken or evaded both as to age and as to hours, not so much in the large factories as in the small workshops which everywhere abound, and in the employment of children at home.' *Report of Committee of Council on Education : J. R. Blakiston's Report : Parl. Pap.* 1875, XXIV, p 258.

[1] Under the Elementary Education Act 1870, which authorized the creation of local school boards with power to make bye-laws in their districts compelling the attendance at school of children.

P

rudiments of learning into the head of a big boy who has just begun to work and earn wages, with only half the number of hours schooling which in other cases is accorded him, is a veritable object of compassion. Nay, more, the provision in the Act of 1874, whereby the age for first employment was raised in textile factories from eight to ten years will operate most detrimentally to the cause of education if it be not supplemented by some provision for securing that the two years thus saved from half-time work shall not be spent in whole-time idleness.' The Commissioners concluded, therefore, that some provision was required, outside the Factory Acts, for enforcing attendance upon the younger children ; and that without this, the existing Factory Act system was, on its educational side, hopelessly deficient. They recommended, also, that the age for entering employment should be raised uniformly to ten years, in support of which they had ' the whole of the staff of Inspectors, the great majority of the employers who have given evidence before us, the medical and educational authorities, and the representative witnesses of the operative class, almost without exception.' While approving the principle of the Act of 1874 of an educational qualification as a condition of transition from half-time to full-time employment, and thinking that provision ought to be made for the gradual application of an educational test, they nevertheless thought that the practical difficulties in the way of operating such a regulation immediately (e.g. the improbability, at the time, of children being able, in general, to reach the ' Fourth Standard ',[1] and the inadequacy of school accommodation) made it undesirable to introduce it at least for some time. With regard to the

[1] *Cf. supra*, p. 207.

amount of attendance to be required under the half-time system, they considered the existing amount, which was equivalent to 220 (half-day) attendances a year, satisfactory.[1]

At this stage, educational legislation and factory legislation made contact with each other. In 1876, there was passed the Elementary Education Act,[2] which dealt with some of the points covered in the Report of the Factory and Workshops Acts Commission. First, by this Act it was declared to be the duty of the parent of every child to cause the child to receive efficient elementary instruction in reading, writing and arithmetic. Secondly, it was forbidden to take into employment any child who was under the age of ten years, or who, being of the age of ten years or upwards, had not obtained either a certificate of proficiency in reading, writing, and elementary arithmetic, or of previous due attendance at a certified efficient school, unless the child was employed and was attending school in accordance with the Factory Acts. Thirdly, as regards children employed in workshops, it was enacted that the provisions respecting education of the Factory Acts 1844 and 1874 should apply to the employment and education of all children employed in factories subject to the Factory Acts 1833 and 1871, and not already subject to the Factory Act 1874, or in workshops subject to the Workshops Act.

It remained to deal with the other recommendations of the Royal Commission and to consolidate the law respecting factories and workshops. Accordingly Assheton Cross, the Home Secretary, introduced a Bill for this purpose

---

[1] *Factory and Workshops Acts Commission : Report : Parl. Pap.* 1876, XXIX, liii-lviii. [2] 39 and 40 Vict., c. 79.

on 6th April, 1877.[1] Though pressure of Parliamentary business rendered progress during that session impossible, the Bill was introduced again at the beginning of 1878,[2] and was passed practically without any opposition ;[3] and thus, at length, employment in factories and that in workshops were brought under the same set of regulations. The consolidated regulations in respect of education provided that :

(1) The parent of a child employed in a factory or in a workshop must cause the child to attend a recognised efficient school for one attendance each working day if employed in a morning or afternoon set, or, if employed on the alternate day system, for two attendances on each work day preceding each day of employment ;

(2) The employer must obtain a school attendance certificate from the teacher of the school respecting the attendance of the child at school in accordance with the Act ;

(3) The managers of the school might apply to the employer to be paid a weekly sum, not exceeding 3d. and not exceeding one-twelfth of the child's wages, to be deducted by the employer from the child's wages ;

(4) When a child of the age of thirteen years had obtained from an authorised person a certificate of having reached a prescribed standard of proficiency in

---

[1] *A Bill to Consolidate and Amend the Law relating to Factories and Workshops : Parl. Pap.* 1877, II, p. 179. *Hansard* 1877, CCXXXIII, p. 756.

[2] *A Bill to Consolidate and Amend the Law relating to Factories and Workshops : Parl. Pap.* 1878, III, p. 1. *Hansard* 1878, CCXXXVII, pp. 155, 1454.

[3] 41 Vict., c. 16.

reading, writing, and arithmetic, or a prescribed standard of previous attendance at a certified efficient school, he should be deemed to be a ' young person ' for the purposes of the Act.

And by this Act, the whole legislation relating to factories and workshops, dealt with in 45 Acts extending over a period of fifty years, was (in the words of Lord Shaftesbury) ' brought into one lucid and harmonious whole . . . in a single statute, simple and intelligible '.[1]

The Factories Inquiry Commissioners of 1833 had said that if the system recommended by them for factory children employed in cotton and woollen mills to attend school so many hours a day should succeed ' it will lay the best foundation for an extended system of education applicable to other classes of infant labourers besides those that are designated by the existing Act, and ultimately perhaps embracing all classes '.[2] Though the foregoing survey shows that the part-time system of education for children engaged in industry made but little real headway in other directions, the influence of the system did in fact extend far beyond the textile trades. The success of the earlier Factory Acts in these industries, qualified though it was on its educational side by the fact that many of the schools were inefficient and that both parents and employers were often indifferent, was the most potent cause of the wide

[1] *Hansard* 1878, CCXXXIX, p. 947.

[2] Factory Inquiries Commission : *Supplementary Report of the Central Board : Parl. Pap.* 1834, XIX, p. 273. It is fitting to mention Lord Shaftesbury's name at the end of this book, for, as has well been said, ' he did more than any single man, or any single Government in English history, to check the raw power of the new industrial system '. *Lord Shaftesbury.* Hammond, J. L. and B. (1923), p. 153.

extension in the sixties and seventies of the regulation of child employment and helped to pave the way for the eventual provision for universal compulsory education.

BIBLIOGRAPHY

I PARLIAMENTARY PAPERS

Report of Minutes of Evidence respecting the state of health and morals of children employed in manufactories ; chiefly as to cotton factories, 1816, III.

Reports from the Select Committee on Artizans and Machinery, 1824, V.

Reports from the Select Committee on the Bill for the regulation of factories, 1831-32, XV.

Report from the Select Committee on Manufactories, Commerce and Shipping, 1833, VI.

First Report from Commissioners appointed to collect information in the manufacturing districts, relative to the employment of children in factories ; with Minutes of Evidence and Reports of District Commissioners, 1833, XX.

Second Report of same, 1833, XXI.

Supplementary Reports of same, 1834, XIX, XX.

Reports from each of the four factory inspectors on the educational provisions of the Factory Act, together with a joint report, 1839, XLII.

Reports from the Assistant Handloom Commissioners, 1840, XXIII, XXIV.

Reports from the Select Committee on the Act for the regulation of factories, together with Minutes of Evidence, 1840, X, 1841, IX

Report of R. J. Saunders upon the establishment of schools in the factory districts, in February, 1842, 1843, XXVII.

First Report of Commissioners for inquiring into the employment of children in mines and manufactories [Mines], 1842, XV.

Reports and evidence of Sub-Commissioners on same, 1842, XVI, XVII.

Second Report of the Commissioners on same [*Trades and Manufactures*], 1843, XIII.

Appendix to same, with Reports and Evidence from Sub-Commissioners, 1843, XIV, XV.

Report of Commissioner on the advisability of extending the provisions of the Acts for the regulation of Mills and Factories to Bleaching Works, 1854-55, XVIII.

Reports of the Select Committee on the employment of women and children in Bleaching and Dyeing Works, 1857 (Sess. 2), XI ; 1857-58, XI.

Report upon the expediency of subjecting Lace Manufacture to the regulations of the Factory Acts, 1861, XXII.

Reports of Commissioners on the employment of children in Trades and Manufactures not already regulated by law : First, 1863, XVIII ; Second and Third, 1864, XXII ; Fourth, 1865, XX ; Fifth, 1866, XXIV ; Sixth, 1867, XVI.

Report by Mr Tremenheere and Mr Tuffnell on Printworks Act and on Bleaching and Dyeing Works Act, 1868-69, XIV.

Report of Commissioners on the working of the Factory and Workshops Acts, with a view to their consolidation and amendment, 1876, XXIX, XXX.

Reports of Inspectors of Factories (*from* 1834).

Report from the Committee appointed to inquire into the present state of Agriculture, 1833.

Reports of Special Poor Law Commissioners on the employment of Women and Children in Agriculture, 1843, XLI.

Sixth Report of Children's Employment Commissioners (*on organized agricultural gangs*), 1867, XVI.

Reports of Commissioners on the Employment of Children, etc., in Agriculture, 1867-68, XVII ; 1868-69, XIII ; 1870, XIII.

First Report of Commissioners for inquiring into the employment of children in mines and manufactories [*Mines*] 1842, XV.

Reports and Evidence of Sub-Commissioners for same, 1842, XVI, XVII.

Report from the Select Committee on Accidents in Mines, 1835, V.

First Report of the Midland Mining Commission, 1843, XIII.

Report of Select Committee of House of Lords on Accidents in Mines, 1849, VII.

Copy of Royal Commission issued to inquire into the condition of Mines to which the provisions of the Act 23 and 24 Vict., c. 151 *do not apply,* 1862, *LV.*
Reports of Commissioners on same, 1864, *XXIV, Parts I and II.*
Report of Select Committee on Mines Inspection, 1865, *XII ;* 1866, *XIV ;* 1867, *XII.*
Annual Reports of the Commissioner appointed under the provisions of the Act 5 and 6 Vict., c. 99 *to inquire into the working of that Act, and into the state of the population in the mining districts (Annually* 1844-1859).
Annual Reports of Inspectors of Mines (from 1854).

Reports from the Select Committee on the state of education among the lower orders, 1816, *IV ;* 1817, *III ;* 1818, *IV.*
Digest of Returns to Circulars from the Committee of the state of schools and means of parochial instruction, 1819, *IX.*
General Table, showing the state of education in England, 1820, *XII.*
Report from the Select Committee on the State of Education, with the Minutes of Evidence, 1834, *IX ;* 1835, *VII ;* 1837-38, *VII.*
Abstract of answers and returns relative to the state of education in England and Wales, 1835, *XLI, XLII, XLIII.*
Report of Commissioners on Popular Education in England ; Reports of Assistant Commissioners ; Minutes of Evidence, 1861, *XXI, Parts I, II, III, IV, V, VI.*
Reports of Committee of Council on Education (with Reports of H.M. Inspectors of Schools).

II HISTORIES—GENERAL AND ECONOMIC

British History in the Nineteenth Century	Trevelyan, G. M.	1922
A History of the English People in 1815 (Translated from the French)	Halévy, E.	1924
A History of the English People in 1815-1830 (Translated from the French) . .	Halévy, E.	1926
A History of the English People in 1830-1841 (Translated from the French) . .	Halévy, E.	1927
Cambridge Modern History, vols, X, XI . . .		1907–09
The History of England during the Reign of Victoria . .	Low, S. & Sanders, L. C.	1907

The Story of the People of England in the Nineteenth Century	McCarthy, J.	1899
A History of England from the Conclusion of the Great War in 1815 [*to* 1858], 5 vols. .	Walpole, S.	1907
A History of Twenty-five Years : 1856-1880, 4 vols. . .	Walpole, S.	1904
The Making of Modern England	Slater, G.	1913
Lectures on the Industrial Revolution in England . .	Toynbee, A.	1908
Life and Labour in the Nineteenth Century . . .	Fay, C. R.	1920
England on the Eve of the Industrial Revolution . .	Moffitt, L. W.	1925
Industrial Society in England towards the end of the Eighteenth Century . .	Bowden, W.	1925
An Economic History of Modern Britain, vol I : *The Early Railway Age* . . .	Clapham, J. H.	1926
The Growth of English Industry and Commerce, 6th edition, 2 vols	Cunningham, W.	1915-19
The Industrial Revolution in the Eighteenth Century (Translated from French) . .	Mantoux, P.	1928
Industrial and Commercial Revolutions in Great Britain in the Nineteenth Century .	Knowles, L.	1921
The Village Labourer . .	Hammond, J. L. & B.	1913
The Town Labourer . .	Hammond, J. L. & B.	1917
The Skilled Labourer . .	Hammond, J. L. & B.	1919
The Rise of Modern Industry .	Hammond, J. L. & B.	1926
The Age of the Chartists . .	Hammond, J. L. & B.	1930
Victorian Working Women, 1832-67	Neff, W. F.	1929
Women Workers and the Industrial Revolution, 1750-1850 .	Pinchbeck, I.	1930
Commerce and Industry : a historical review, 1815-1914, 2 vols. . . .	Page, W. (Ed.)	1919
Economic Annals of the Nineteenth Century, 2 vols. . .	Smart, W.	1910-17
Industry in England : Historical Outlines (11th Edition) .	Gibbins, H. de B.	1929

English Poor Law History, Part I, to 1834. Part II, The Last Hundred Years . .	Webb, S. &. B.	1926–29
Health, Wealth and Population, 1760-1815 . . .	Buer, M.	1926
History of Labour . .	Stone, G.	1921
The Worker and the State .	Tillyard, F.	1923
Labour Migration 1800-1850 .	Redford, A.	1926
English Apprenticeship and Child Labour . . .	Dunlop, O. J. & Denman, R. D.	1912
History of English Philanthropy	Gray, K.	1905
Progress of the Working Class in the Last Half Century .	Giffen, R.	1884

III HISTORY OF FACTORY LEGISLATION

The Factories Regulation Act Explained, with some Remarks on its Origin, Nature, and Tendency . . .	Horner, L.	1834
History of the Factory Movement, 2 vols. . . .	'Alfred' (S. Kydd)	1850
The English Factory Legislation	Von Plener, E.	1873
History of Factory Legislation	Grant, P.	1866
The Law Relating to Factories and Workshops . . .	Notcutt, G. J.	1879
The Factory and Workshop Act, 1878 (2nd Edition) . .	Redgrave, A.	1879
Labour Legislation . .	Howell, G.	1902
Child Labour in the United Kingdom	Keeling, F.	1914
A History of Factory Legislation (3rd Edition) . . .	Hutchins, B. L. & Harrison, A.	1926
Factory Legislation and its Administration, 1891-1924 .	Mess, H. A.	1926

IV HISTORIES OF INDUSTRIES AND TRADES

Compendious History of Cotton Manufacture . . .	Guest, R.	1823
History of the Cotton Manufacture	Baines, E., Jr.	1835
Cotton Manufacture in Great Britain, 2 vols . . .	Ure, A.	1836
The Philosophy of Manufactures	Ure, A.	1835

The Early English Cotton Industry . . .	Daniels, G. W.	1920
The Lancashire Cotton Industry	Chapman, S. J.	1904
History of Machine - wrought Hosiery and Lace Manufacture	Felkin, W.	1867
A History of Bleaching . .	Higgins, S. H.	1924
The Cutlery Trades . .	Lloyd, G. I. H.	1913
Comprehensive History of the Woollen and Worsted Manufactures, 2 vols . .	Bischoff, J.	1842
The Yorkshire Woollen and Worsted Industries . .	Heaton, H.	1920
The Woollen and Worsted Industries	Clapham, J. H.	1907
The History of the Woollen and Worsted Industries . .	Lipson, E.	1921
History of Coal Mining in Great Britain	Galloway, R. L.	1882
Coal Mines Inspection: Its History and Results . .	Boyd, R. W.	1879
History of the Coal Trade .	Boyd, R.	1892
The British Coal Trade .	Jevons, H. S.	1915
The Rise of the English Coal Industry (shortly). .	Nef, J. U.	1931
History of the Iron Trade .	Scrivenor, H.	1854
Iron and Steel in the Industrial Revolution . . .	Ashton, T. S.	1924
English Farming, Past and Present . . .	Prothero, R. E.	1912
A History of the English Agricultural Labourer (Translated from German) . . .	Hasbach, W.	1908

V CONTEMPORARY LITERATURE

A New View of Society and Other Writings (Everyman Library Edition, 1927) . . .	Owen, R.	1813–14
An Examination of the Cotton Factory Question .		1819
Abstract of the Evidence given to the Committee of the House of Lords, Appointed to Inquire into the State and Condition of Children Employed in Cotton Factories . . .		1819

Answers to Certain Objections made to Sir Robert Peel's Bill for Ameliorating the Condition of Children Employed in Cotton Factories. . . .		1819
An Enquiry into the State of the Manufacturing Population .		1831
Evils of the Factory System .	Wing, C.	1837
A Letter to Lord Althorp in Defence of the Cotton Factories of Lancashire . . .	Hoole, H.	1832
A Letter to Mr Holland Hoole in Reply to his Letter to Lord Althorp	Oastler, R.	1832
The Moral and Physical Condition of the Working Classes Employed in the Cotton Manufacture in Manchester .	Kay, J. P.	1832
History of the Middle and Working Classes (2nd Edition) .	Wade, J.	1834
Factory Statistics . .	Sadler, M. T.	1836
Curse of the Factory System .	Fielden, J.	1836
The Factory Question and the Ten Hours Bill . . .	Greg, R. H.	1837
Letters on the Factory Act	Senior, N. W.	1837
Artizans and Machinery : The Moral and Physical Condition of the Manufacturing Population . . .	Gaskell, P.	1836
Arts and Artizans at Home and Abroad	Symons, J. C.	1839
On the Employment of Children in Factories . . .	Horner, L.	1840
State of the Poorer Classes in Great Towns . . .	Slaney, R. A.	1840
The Factory System Illustrated.	Dodd, W. (' A Factory Cripple ')	1842
Notes of a Tour in the Manufacturing Districts of Lancashire	Taylor, W. C.	1842
Letter to Lord Ashley, M.P., on the Mines and Collieries Bill.	Londonderry, Marquis of.	1842
Days at the Factories, or the Manufacturing Industry of Great Britain Described .	Dodd, G.	1843

The Wrongs of Our Youth : An Essay on the Evils of the Late-Hour System . . .	Grindrod, R. B.	1843
The Social, Educational and Religious State of the Manufacturing Districts . .	Baines, E. Jr.	1843
Replies of Sir Charles Shaw to Lord Ashley, M.P., regarding the Education and Moral and Physical Condition of the Labouring Classes . .	Osborne, S. G.	1844
A View of the Low Moral and Physical Condition of the Agricultural Labourer .	Osborne, S. G.	1844
Factories and the Factory System	Taylor, W. C.	1844
Manchester in 1844 : its Present Position and Future Prospects (Translated from French) . . .	Faucher	1844
American Factories : with an Appeal on Behalf of the British Factory Population .	Scoresby, W.	1845
The Claims of Labour : An Essay on the Duties of the Employers to the Employed .	Helps, A.	1845
The Peasantry of England .	Perry, G. W.	1846
On the Condition of the Agricultural Labourer . . .	Nichols, G.	1846
A History of the Past and Present State of the Labouring Population, 2 vols. . .	Tuckett, J. D.	1846
The Labouring Classes in England, especially those engaged in Agriculture and Manufactures.	' An Englishman '	1847
The Social Condition and Education of the People in England and Europe, 2 vols. .	Kay, J.	1850
Our Labouring Classes : Their Intellectual, Moral and Social Condition Considered . .	Couling, S.	1851
Agricultural Labourers, as they Were, Are and Should be, in their Social Condition . .	Stuart, H.	1853

Our Coal and Our Coal Pits: the People in them and the Scenes Around Them. .	' A Traveller Underground '	1853
A Picture of a Manufacturing District	Potter, E.	1856
The Half-Holiday Question, with some Thoughts on the Instruction and Healthful Recreations of the Industrial Classes	Lilwall	1856
Life of Robert Owen, by Himself (Bohn Library Edition 1920)		1857–58
Transactions of the National Association of Coal, Lime, and Iron-stone Miners of Great Britain . . .		1864
Progress of the Working-Class, 1832-67	Ludlow, J. M. & Lloyd Jones	1867
Speeches of the Earl of Shaftesbury upon Subjects Relative Chiefly to the Claims and Interests of the Labouring Classes		1868
The Agricultural Labourer .	Kebbel, T. E.	1870
The English Peasantry . .	Heath, F. G.	1874
History of the Factory System .	Taylor, R. W. C.	1886
Condition of the Working Classes in 1844 (Translated from German)	Engels, F.	1892

VI EDUCATION

Report of a Committee of the Manchester Statistical Society on the State of Education in Manchester . . .		1835
Same on the State of Education in Bury		1835
Same on the State of Education in Liverpool . . .		1836
Same on the State of Education in Salford . . .		1836
Education Reform: or the Necessity of a National System of Education . . .	Wyse, T.	1836

The Central Society of Education, Papers 1837–39		
Recent Measures for the Promoting of Education in England		1840
Elementary Education : the Importance of its Extension in our own Country. . .	Edwards, H.	1844
Popular Education in England.	Vaughan, R.	1846
Letters to Lord John Russell on State Education . . .	Baines, E., Jr.	1846
The Education of the Poor in England and Europe . .	Kay, J.	1846
National Education . .	Dufton, J.	1847
A Plea for Schools . .	Symons, J. C.	1847
Observations on the Working of the Government Scheme of Education. . . .	Dawes, R.	1849
The Condition and Education of Poor Children in English and German Towns . .	Kay, J.	1853
The State of our Educational Enterprises . . .	Fraser, W.	1858
Suggestions on Popular Education	Senior, N. W.	1861
Four Periods of Public Education	Kay-Shuttleworth, J.	1862
The Schools for the People .	Bartley, G. C. T.	1871
The History of the Elementary School Contest in England .	Adams, F.	1882
The State and Education .	Craik, H.	1884
Elementary Education : Some Account of its Rise and Progress in England . .	Gregory, R.	1895
English National Education .	Holman, H.	1898
Reports on Elementary Schools (Reprinted 1908) . .	Arnold, M.	1889
Education in the Nineteenth Century	Roberts, R. O. (Ed.)	1901
State Intervention in English Education, down to 1833 .	Montmorency, J. E. G. de	1902
The Educational Systems of Great Britain and Ireland (2nd Edition) . . .	Balfour, G.	1903
The Progress of Education in England	Montmorency, J. E. G. de	1904

A Century of Education .	Binns, H. B.	1908
A Short History of Education .	Adamson, J. W.	1919
Education and Social Movements, 1700-1850 . .	Dobbs, A. E.	1919
The English Elementary School	Newton, A. W.	1919
History of Elementary Education in England and Wales (2nd Edition) . . .	Birchenough, C.	1925
English Education, 1798-1902 .	Adamson, J. W.	1930

VII BIOGRAPHIES

English Social Reformers (2nd Edition) . . .	Gibbins, H. de B.	1902
Pioneers of Reform . .	Johnson, D. S.	1929
Robert Owen . . .	Cole, G. D. H.	1925
Robert Owen, 2 vols . .	Podmore, F.	1906
Life of Francis Place . .	Wallas, G.	1918
Sir Robert Peel, 3 vols .	Parker, C. S.	1899
Sir Robert Peel . . .	Ramsay, A. A. M.	1927
Life and Letters of Sir James Graham, 2 vols . . .	Parker, C. S.	1907
Life of Lord John Russell, 2 vols.	Walpole, S.	1889
Memoir of Viscount Althorp, Third Earl Spencer . .	Le Marchant, D.	1876
The Life and Work of the Seventh Earl of Shaftesbury, 3 vols .	Hodder, E.	1886
Life of Lord Shaftesbury . .	Hammond, J. L. & B.	1923
Lord Shaftesbury . . .	Bready, J. W.	1926
Lord Brougham and the Whig Party	Aspinall, A.	1927
The Life and Works of Sir James Kay-Shuttleworth .	Smith, F.	1923
Life of W. E. Forster . .	Reid, T. W.	1889
Life of Henry Fawcett (5th Edition) . . .	Stephens, H.	1886
Sir Edwin Chadwick . .	Marston, M.	1925

INDEX

229

For Product Safety Concerns and Information please contact our EU
representative GPSR@taylorandfrancis.com
Taylor & Francis Verlag GmbH, Kaufingerstraße 24, 80331 München, Germany